Hiring Data Scientists and Machine Learning Engineers

A Practical Guide

Roy Keyes

Hiring Data Scientists and Machine Learning Engineers
A Practical Guide

Roy Keyes

ISBN 9781637905258

If you purchased this paperback, you can get a free copy of the ebook by going to dshiring.com/companioncopy

More info can be found at dshiring.com

This book was created on Leanpub (leanpub.com).

Contents

Acknowledgements   1

Chapter 1: Introduction   3
    What is this book?   3
    Who is this book for?   4
    Why is this book needed?   5
    Why is this book any good?   6

Chapter 2: What is data science and machine learning? .   7
    What is data science and who is a data scientist?   7
    What is machine learning and machine learning engi-
        neering? 14
    Wrapping up 19

Interview: Julie Hollek, Mozilla 21

Chapter 3: Determining what roles you need 31
    Defining your business goal 31
    How do data science and machine learning fit in? 32
    Defining the roles you need 35
    The many roles in data science 35
    Determining the roles you need 38
    Determining job titles for new roles 48
    Wrapping up: Roles 49

Interview: Chris Albon, Wikimedia 51

Chapter 4: Creating a hiring strategy **59**

Determining your resources and constraints 60

Understanding the job market 63

Scaling to meet your expected applicant volume 66

Determining your recruiting strategy 68

Structuring your hiring process 72

Making decisions 76

Summary 81

Interview: Sean Taylor, Lyft **83**

Chapter 5: Job descriptions and resumes **91**

Writing an effective job description 92

Reviewing resumes 98

Summary 104

Interview: Angela Bassa, iRobot **105**

Chapter 6: Technical skills assessment **117**

Skills assessment 117

What does it mean to assess technical skills? 118

How can you assess technical skills? 120

What are we trying to assess? 120

Methods for skills assessment 122

Creating a fair skills assessment 126

Deciding on your strategy 127

Which skills should you be assessing? 128

Choosing assessment material 130

Assessing your assessment material 131

Scoring and decision making 133

The life cycle of your assessments 136

Considerations for "live" skills assessments 137

Summary 138

Interview: Ravi Mody, Spotify **139**

Chapter 7: Interviewing **149**
    The goals of the interview process 149
    When to do which interviews 151
    What should you be assessing during an interview? . . . 153
    Interviewing strategy 153
    Interviewing logistics and decision making 155
    How do you know if your hiring process is succeeding? 159
    Summary 161

Chapter 8: Setting up your team for success **163**
    Structuring your team 163
    Onboarding new hires 166
    Care and feeding of data scientists and MLE's 168
    Summary 172

Appendices **173**
    Appendix I: Task and skills breakdowns, with associated
        roles 173
    Appendix II: Skills of different roles 178

Summary and Cheat Sheet **195**
    Steps to effective DS/MLE hiring 195

Acknowledgements

This book would not exist without the support and assistance of a number of people.

I would like to first thank the people I interviewed for this book: Julie Hollek, Chris Albon, Sean Taylor, Angela Bassa, and Ravi Mody.

I would also like to thank all of the people who contributed to this book in numerous other ways: J.J., A.B., I.P., B.E., A.M., J.A., N.K., D.T.S., J.G., V.B., J.J., T.W. (and a few that I'm sure I've forgotten [you know who you are]).

Finally I would like to thank all of the people who pre-purchased this book and especially those early readers who sent me feedback and questions.

And of course you, the reader! Thank you.

Chapter 1: Introduction

$$f(x) = \begin{cases} 0 & \text{if } x < 0 \\ x & \text{if } x \geq 0 \end{cases}$$

$$f'(x) = \begin{cases} 0 & \text{if } x < 0 \\ 1 & \text{if } x \geq 0 \end{cases}$$

In the past fifteen years, data (big, small, and in between) has taken on a new importance as a core asset and enabler across industries, scientific pursuits, government, and many other areas of society. In business, the ability to extract value from that data has become a necessity rather than something exotic or simply a nice-to-have.

To extract the value from your business' data, you need the right people. Hiring the right people to do that is what this book is about.

What is this book?

This book is designed to be a concise, opinionated, and practical guide to hiring the right data science technologists that your organization needs to achieve its goals. It will guide you through identifying the roles and skills your organization needs, how to source candidates, how to assess candidates, and how to help them succeed once hired. At each step, the book will try to give you a clear set of criteria and choices to create the most effective and efficient hiring process.

This book also has several interviews with data science and machine learning engineering hiring managers from some of the major internet companies. These interviews offer a broad perspective on the challenges of hiring, along with an inside view into how managers at these companies try to address them.

Who is this book for?

This book is aimed at anyone who wants to build or grow a data science or machine learning team. This may be the CEO of a small startup, a new manager at a large tech company, the leader of a new data-driven project at a non-profit, or the head of "digital transformation" at a massive global industrial company. While the needs and available resources across organizations vary greatly, this book aims to provide a useful framework and game plan adaptable to many different scenarios.

Different readers will come into this book with differing levels of experience related to hiring, data science, and machine learning engineering. Accordingly, some material can be skipped, depending on your background and experience. If you are a data scientist who has been through the hiring process on the candidate side of the table, you'll understand a lot of the pitfalls and difficulties with data science skills and fit assessment, but may be unfamiliar with the logistics and challenges of the overall hiring process. If you have hired lots of people before, but have never hired a machine learning engineer, you'll be familiar with the general hiring process, but may not have experience with the specifics of creating an MLE job description or what to look for in a candidate.

Some material in this book will be more relevant to companies in the United States rather than non-profits, government agencies, or non-US organizations. I will try to note material, such as employment law related information, as being specific to the US or American corporations[1].

---

[1]Be on the lookout for footnotes.

Why is this book needed?

Data science and machine learning have exploded in popularity in recent years. The sudden popularity and prominence, along with the hope and hype accompanying this explosion, have left many very excited about the promise of data science, but unsure how to get the expected value for their organization. As with any rapidly emerging new field, it's not always clear what skills and qualifications a practitioner needs. The plethora of new boot camps, degree programs, and online courses has helped the potential workforce grow very rapidly, but also created a situation where it's still unclear who is best suited for a given role. This means that hiring managers often find themselves in the situation of dealing with an overwhelmingly large number of job applicants with no clear way to filter on the best candidates.

While there are many resources out there for aspiring data scientists looking for jobs, there are few aimed at those who need to hire data scientists and machine learning engineers. The hope is that this book can fulfill some of that need. To that end, this book aims to clarify your organization's needs, while guiding your hiring journey to reduce confusion and increase hiring effectiveness and efficiency.

A note on my background

The majority of my hands-on hiring experience has been in the setting of small to medium sized tech startups. The primary thing that those settings all had common was a low level of resources for hiring and the tendency towards hiring generalists, who could adapt to the rapidly changing needs of the organization. Because of that, some of the advice in this book will be biased towards that situation.

In the parts of the book where we talk about hiring strategy and needs, I will specifically discuss how to think about your available resources and the difference between having generalists versus specialists on your team. Additionally, the hiring manager interviews interspersed throughout the book will add different perspectives on the challenges, strategies, and goals of hiring data scientists and machine learning engineers.

Why is this book any good?

There's no guarantee that this book will lead you to where you need or want to be, but the hope is that it will at least get you close. While this is an opinionated book offering some specific recommendations, there is no such thing as one-size-fits-all in hiring. Nonetheless, I hope that the specific recommendations made will be highly valuable to most readers, but even more importantly that the questions posed to you will put you on the path to hiring success.

In the tech world, hiring and interviewing is a topic that is sure to spark disagreement and endless discussion. It's probably safe to say that no one has solved hiring (a fact that I will repeat throughout this book!). In fact, there are probably many reasonable approaches, a few good approaches, and very few, if any, great approaches to general hiring. Hopefully the questions, guidance, and recommendations in this book will move you much closer to the best hiring approach for your organization's specific hiring scenario.

Chapter 2: What is data science and machine learning?

$$\min_{w \in R^d} \frac{1}{n} \|y - X w\|_{R^n}^2 + \lambda \|w\|_{R^d}^2$$

Data science is as wonderful as it is ambiguous. If you ask ten data scientists what exactly data science is, you are likely to get ten answers different enough to leave you wondering if data science really exists as "a thing". In this chapter we'll cover some of the basic themes and common definitions behind data science, machine learning, and machine learning engineering. While you will not come away with the "one, true" definitions of these, hopefully you will feel that you have a better grasp of how these terms are used.

This chapter covers background information that data science and machine learning practitioners can safely skip, though hopefully you'll find something of interest.

What is data science and who is a data scientist?

Very broadly, data science[2] is the application of computational and statistical methods to data in order to answer questions, make

---

[2]For most of this book I will use "data science" in a very broad sense, encompassing a wide range of activities and roles, including machine learning. As will be discussed in later chapters, some organizations use the term "data science" in a much narrower context.

predictions, and automate tasks. One way to break down data science is to look at the kinds of things data scientists typically do.

Two types of data science activities

1) Data analysis

One broad category of data science activity is performing data analysis to answer questions. Questions that data scientist seek to answer could include:

- Is product version A superior to product version B?
- How do the different components of our system or process affect the outcome?
- How can we best measure our performance?

These types of problems are often addressed with statistical and analytical techniques. The output is typically a report or a dashboard.

2) Data products

Another broad category of data science activity is building data-driven functionality into products. Examples of this include:

- Recommendations systems
- Search engines
- Arrival time estimates
- Automated demand forecasting
- Ad placement

These types of problems are often addressed with machine learning or other statistical modeling techniques.

Both categories require supporting infrastructure and activities, such as data collection, data engineering, software engineering, and devops. How all of these fit together will be discussed more in the chapter on defining roles.

Data science tasks

Data science is a set of techniques and technologies used to solve business problems, which are ultimately what an organization cares about. To solve a given business problem a data science team typically needs to carry out a very wide range of tasks. Some of those tasks include:

- Finding and collecting data
- Cleaning data
- Exploring data
- Building data transformation pipelines
- Formulating metrics
- Creating reports
- Creating dashboards
- Designing and interpreting experiments
- Developing predictive models, e.g. machine learning models
- Deploying predictive models
- Maintaining predictive models
- Creating web apps and APIs
- Communicating with stakeholders (internal or external)
- Fixing problems in any of the above

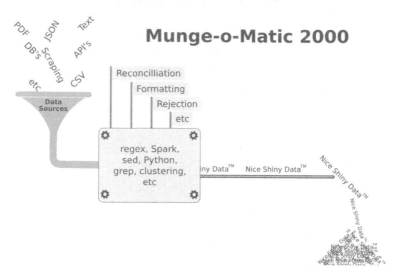

Data scientists and data engineers spend much of their time on data preparation

As you can imagine, many data scientists have knowledge of all of these tasks, but very few have substantive experience with the full range. How these tasks and responsibilities are typically broken down is something that will be discussed later.

Why is data science happening now?

While people have been undertaking similar approaches to problem solving since the advent of the computer, the modern discipline under the moniker of "data science" emerged at the end of the 2000's in the tech world. Data science came about as the methodology to generate value from so-called "big data", which was a description of the suddenly large amount of data being generated from mobile devices, social media, and other sources.

Several related trends were driving the growth of data and the ability to handle it at scale. The explosion of data has been driven by the continued growth of internet use, especially via mobile phones, adoption of social media, and the growth of the internet of things. This growth was in part enabled by the cost of data storage, processing, and bandwidth dropping exponentially, following trends similar to Moore's Law[3] [4] [5] [6]. At the same time open source software to handle and analyze big data was picking up steam - in particular Hadoop and the R and Python ecosystems. The open publication of new techniques enabled rapid advances by the community and incorporation of new methods into freely available software. Additionally, the rise of cloud computing put this all in reach of even relatively small businesses.

In the late 2000's and early 2010's the term "data scientist" started to become popularized. Early successes at companies such as LinkedIn (e.g. the People You May Know feature) and OKCupid fueled interest in the idea that businesses could apply statistical techniques to the data that they were already collecting for their day-to-day operations and extract additional value. Articles making lofty proclamations, such as "the sexy job in the next 10 years will be statisticians"[7] or even loftier, such as data science being the "sexiest job of the 21st century"[8], drove the interest in data science as a career and promoted the idea that there would be an extreme shortage of people with the needed skills.

Who is a data scientist?

Because data science is still a new and emerging field, the educational background and qualifications of a data scientist are not necessarily clear cut. Being such a new profession, until recently all data scientists were necessarily coming from other fields. In the early days a lot of those people were coming from scientific

---

[3] https://en.wikipedia.org/wiki/Moore%27s_law
[4] Data Age 2025, IDC
[5] A history of storage cost, mkomo
[6] 42 Years of Microprocessor Trend Data, Karl Rupp
[7] For Today's Graduate, Just One Word: Statistics
[8] Data Scientist: The Sexiest Job of the 21st Century

fields, such as physics. Fields that already involved a lot of statistical thinking, question answering, and computing were fertile grounds for finding potential data scientists.

Does a data scientist need to have a PhD?

There are a lot of data scientists that have PhD's and it is a common question whether a PhD is needed to be a data scientist. I think the answer is pretty clearly "no".

A PhD is a degree designed to train people in doing academic research. Academic research is very different from what most data scientists typically do (aside from those in academia). There are in fact successful data scientists in the business world that came into the field without even having obtained undergraduate degrees. That said, the skills that PhD students in several fields learn and practice have large amounts of overlap with the skills needed by data scientists. Arguably the number one skill for data scientists is being able to rapidly learn new techniques, technologies, and domains, something the PhD students are typically good at.

For some very specialized data science roles, especially roles with the expectation of publishing lots of research, a PhD is probably an appropriate qualification. Even then, it is not necessarily required, depending on experience and aptitude.

Nowadays there are many routes to data science, some more "official" than others. A student can now receive both undergraduate and graduate degrees in data science from reputable universities. Online courses, both paid and free, are ubiquitous[9] [10]. There are also many data science "boot camps", which purport to train people up in a few weeks.

[9]Machine Learning by Stanford University
[10]Practical Deep Learning for Coders

Like many other fields of technology data science has evolved very quickly. It's arguable that the foundations and basics are still up in the air and may take a while to solidify, if ever. New university-based programs have made progress in preparing students, but the field itself has also progressed in that time and remains a moving target. Ultimately data scientists have to fill in the gaps via self-study and on-the-job learning.

Which academic fields do data scientists typically study?

More and more new graduates are coming into data science with degrees specifically in data science, machine learning, or analytics, but other related fields that are heavy on math and computing are often what data scientists have studied. Typical fields of study include, but are not limited to:

- Computer science
- Statistics
- Mathematics
- Physical sciences
- Engineering
- Biological sciences
- Psychology and cognitive science
- Quantitatively focused social sciences (e.g. economics)

Ultimately anyone with the right skills, experience, and the ability to keep up with the latest developments in the field can be a data scientist. No specific degree or qualification is required.

What is machine learning and machine learning engineering?

Machine learning (ML) is one of the most common techniques employed by data scientists. It can be thought of as a way to create software functionality, where the decision logic is not hand-coded by a programmer, but rather the software "learns" the decision logic by looking at lots of data examples.

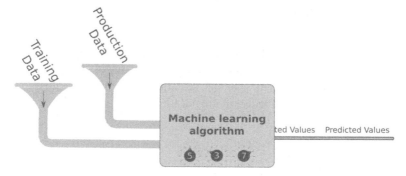

Machine learning algorithms learn to predict using training data

Machine learning is used across a very wide range of applications. Some typical examples of problems solved (fully or partially) with machine learning include:

- Image recognition and classification
    - Face recognition
    - Automated radiology
    - Detecting illegal logging activity in satellite images
- Price and demand forecasting
- Product recommendations
- Self-driving vehicles and robotics
- Credit scoring and risk prediction
- Customer segmentation and targeted marketing

- Search engines
- Customer support routing and triage
- Natural language processing
  - Translation
  - Text generation
  - Voice transcription
- Image transformation and generation
  - Image colorization
  - "Snapchat filters"
  - Face generation
- Music generation
- Game play
  - Board games, such as Go and Chess
  - Video games, such as Atari games and Starcraft

One common way to categorize machine learning techniques is by splitting them into supervised learning and unsupervised learning categories, depending on how data is used in training the model. Supervised learning uses "labeled" data for model training. That means in the example data, the answer, or quantity of interest, is known. This is the label. For example, if you are training a model to predict real estate resale values, if you know the price of past sales, you can use that data in a supervised manner, where the price is the label. The model training process consists of adjusting parameters within the model and comparing the models output. This is done in an automated fashion.

Unsupervised learning is the set of techniques typically applied to data without labels. Examples of this include grouping customers into groups, based on purchasing behavior, or grouping songs into genres. Which group a customer belongs in or which genre(s) a song belongs in are not necessarily known at the outset.

There are other techniques that fall in between these two categories, such as semi-supervised learning and self-supervised learning.

Another way to categorize problems solved with ML is breaking them into regression and classification problems. Regression is a supervised technique used when the quantity of interest is a continuous or nearly continuous numerical value, such as a price. Classification is when the quantity of interest is discrete and unordered, such as determining whether an email is spam.

Examples of regression problems include

- Forecasting tomorrow's outdoor temperature
- Predicting the sales price of a house
- Credit scoring
- Predicting the distance from the camera to an object in an image
- Estimated time of arrival

Examples of classification problems include

- Finger print identification
- Language detection in text
- Spam detection
- Detecting a tumor in a CT scan
- Birdcall identification

Some problems, such as building recommendation systems, can be addressed with regression and/or classification-based strategies, depending on the specifics.

What about artificial intelligence?

Artificial intelligence (AI) is the use of computers to perform activities that require human or animal levels of intelligence. Historically, tasks such as playing chess, image recognition, and text generation have been placed in this category. Currently the primary technique used for AI is machine learning and closely related techniques.

> While a lot of the recent hype has been about AI and its promise, for the most part, ML is the more specific term for the techniques and skills that organizations are focused on, with the exception of the marketing departments.

Machine learning engineering

While machine learning is one of the techniques used by data scientists, machine learning in production systems is often complicated enough that it requires a more specialized set of skills to deploy and manage the system at scale. This role is typically labeled machine learning engineering (MLE).

MLE's tend to focus on some or all of

- Developing ML models
- Data engineering
- Deploying ML models
- Managing and maintaining ML models
- Building and maintaining tools and infrastructure for the above

While MLE is a newer role than data scientist and typically has a more narrowly defined scope, the role can also vary considerably from organization to organization. On some teams the MLE will act in a full-stack capacity, developing, deploying, and managing models end-to-end. In other organizations the model may be developed by someone else, such as a data scientist or even a "machine learning modeler", and the MLE may focus only on model deployment and monitoring or related infrastructure.

There is a lack of agreement on what MLE is

Some (anonymous) quotes.

On the confusion around who does what:

> We have an SWE[a] team that's building an ML
> platform and DS are responsible for full cycle
> (research through productionization and mainte-
> nance). We don't have any formal MLE roles and
> nobody can agree on what an MLE is. The SWE's
> are like, "we're the MLE's" and the data scientists,
> who end up doing a lot of the engineering work,
> say "we're the MLE's".

On the provenance of the title:

> Once DS became a job title that companies gave
> to Data Analysts, MLE was created to give a job
> title to people working on the original promise of
> DS.

_____

[a]Software engineering

Machine learning engineering is often seen in more mature, production oriented settings, where uptime, scale, and lifecycle management are as important as the model's predictive performance.
Typically these teams include other engineering heavy roles.

Who is a machine learning engineer?

Like the role of data scientist, the background of MLE's is not uniform. Many MLE's started as data scientists and gravitated towards
the more engineering-centric aspects of ML model deployment.
This is often a natural consequence of building models end-to-end

and finding yourself spending a lot of time on the production aspects. Other MLE's may have come from the software engineering side of things and taken an interest in ML and supporting ML in production.

As previously mentioned, MLE can vary considerably depending on the organization. For MLE roles that have a stronger focus on model development, a background more similar to a typical DS is expected. For MLE roles that are more focused on system design, infrastructure, and operations, less knowledge of ML algorithms may be sufficient. Typically MLE's need to have very solid software development skills, including setting up and operating cloud-based serving and monitoring infrastructure. Compared to data scientists, MLE are more likely to have a traditional CS background. As with data scientists, ultimately anyone with the right skills and experience can work as an MLE, regardless of educational background.

Wrapping up

Data science is a broad set of data-centric approaches used to solve a diverse set of problems. Machine learning is one subset of those techniques that has enjoyed increasing popularity and success in the last decade. Because data science is a wide-ranging and relatively new field, data scientists come from a wide variety of backgrounds. No single educational background is required, rather the ability to perform the tasks of data science and the ability to consistently learn new skills are the primary requisites. While data scientists often work on machine learning, machine learning engineers specialize more narrowly on various aspects of machine learning, from model development to model deployment and maintenance.

Interview: Julie Hollek, Mozilla

Julie Hollek is a Senior Data Science Manager at Mozilla. She previously held a similar role at Twitter. Prior to working in data science, she completed a PhD in astronomy.

In the interview below, she discusses some of the main challenges faced by data science hiring managers and some of the approaches that she has used to address those challenges.

Roy: Let's start off by having you tell us some about your background and current role.

Julie: I'm a Senior Data Science Manager at Mozilla. I've been at Mozilla since January 2020, where I lead the DS efforts around our business. That means revenue, metrics, and KPI's around how we make money. Before that I was at Twitter for about three and a half years, where my main focus was internet health and safety. I started as an individual contributor and grew into a manger there. That's where I started getting deeply involved in hiring in the first place. Before that I was an IC at an ad tech company. And prior to that I did a coding boot camp. Before all of that I did my PhD at the University of Texas, Austin, studying astronomy.

Roy: What kind of roles have you mostly hired for?

Julie: I've been a hiring manager primarily for DS roles. In this case mostly product data science, looking at how the product is performing, what are the metrics that make sense to measure, how do you think creatively about opportunity sizing, and those types of things. I've also been involved on hiring panels for other positions like product managers and director of data science roles, but primarily I've been involved in hiring individual contributors for data science.

Roy: How did you learn how to hire?

Julie: It was partly baptism by fire and partly learning company rituals, but I think it was a good experience. The company rituals are "this is how we do hiring" and "this is our scoring system", basically what they see as the "right" way to hire. While I was at Twitter, a lot of those things were being built out broadly. I think those were a really good place to start. They were built with things like diversity, equity, and inclusion in mind, which I think are really critical. What I think is interesting is that, as I was starting to hire folks, these weren't standard yet, so there was a lot of kind of playing it by ear.

Twitter and Mozilla, even more so, are engineering companies and are engineering led on the technical side. That means that these processes are built out for engineers. I don't think it's always a one-to-to, where you can just swap out the hiring process for engineers for hiring data scientists, but a lot of the same approach can be used. A lot of how I approach hiring was starting with that framework. For example, when you ask questions, you should have a rubric to make sure everyone on the hiring panel knows what they're looking for. Implicit bias is something that everyone has and you can't really get rid of it, so a lot of the hiring practices that were developed at Twitter I've tried to bring with me to Mozilla. Part of that is about how you interrupt bias and how you make sure that you're asking the candidates questions that are most relevant to the actual role.

I think in a way, that hiring for technical roles is fundamentally broken, because the tests that are used to screen applicants don't really reflect the day-to-day work. For example, there's no world where reversing a linked list on a whiteboard will help you with a business decision. It's just not gonna happen. But you still see that kind of thing in so many interviews. How do you take that out and actually get at the thing you are testing for and understand how someone would apply that knowledge?

Roy: What do you see as the biggest challenges in hiring data scientists?

Julie: I think that there are a few different big challenges. One is "how do you test the thing that you actually want to test" to know that someone will actually be a successful data scientist. For example, if you look at grad school, people have studied the GRE for years and found that "oopsies, this doesn't really tell us anything". Even though I scored poorly on the Physics GRE, I was still able to get a PhD in a physics field, because it didn't actually test everything needed. The problem with tests in the hiring process is that they tend to fall into this "GRE trap".

Mozilla has a very interesting interview process. For IC's you simulate a day of work and try to understand how they would perform. It comes much closer to figuring our how someone will do here, because so much of being a data scientist is basically "how well can you Google this problem?" and "how well can you read the Pandas documentation?". That kind of work is a big part of getting the job done. It's hard to test for that based on first principles approaches.

Roy: I agree. I've come to the view that the most import skill is the ability to learn, where part of that is having the tenacity to just push through and also realizing that there will be so many new things that you don't know and that you need to learn.

Julie: Yes, and I think it's really hard to test that with a coding problem or even a case study. It's more like "once you've been working on this project for two weeks and keep running into the same error" or "why is this number three times larger than it's supposed to be?". Figuring out how people react to those situations is really hard to test.

I think the other big challenge in hiring is building diverse teams. At Mozilla, for example, as a data scientist you're helping making decisions that impact a lot of people that you don't actually know. So it's incredibly important to have a very diverse team with different view points. You probably can't have a team that's just from the same three schools. You have to have some variety of people with different backgrounds and different lived experiences.

Roy: Is the challenge getting that team or having that team?

Julie: It's both. It's really easy to source all of your buddies, who tend to be very similar to you. In order to find people who are invested enough in your company to want to work for you and bring a diversity of perspective, it takes a lot of work. You really need to lay the ground work for this years before hand. It's suspicious when a company comes to organizations meant for under-represented folks and says, "Guess what? We're hiring!". It doesn't feel very trustworthy. You need to build community and building community is something that companies don't typically put enough stock in when they think about hiring, in particular.

Roy: It feels artificial, like "we have an OKR that says this!".

Julie: Yes, exactly. It doesn't necessarily make people feel included or that their experience at work will be awesome. It makes them feel like they're just being hired to fill a quota for the year.

Roy: You started in data science in 2015. That sounds like a short amount of time, but in data science years that's like a lifetime. What have you seen that's changed in that time?

Julie: When I say "software engineer", you don't know what I mean. You need more information. You need "frontend", "backend", "fullstack", etc. There are all of these modifiers. I think data science hasn't gotten there, but it's getting close. You see this some in the differentiation of titles. There's "data scientist", but now there's also "machine learning engineer", so the industry is starting to differentiate. It makes sense.

In machine learning in industry, I believe that fundamentally the most difficult part is actually the infrastructure. It's not about training the model. Anybody can train a model. The challenging parts are understanding whether the model makes any sense and how you serve it to possibly millions of users.

Roy: There are so many things that need to happen to get a model into production. Otherwise your model will just end up in some slidedeck or a notebook that maybe you show to someone.

Julie: Exactly. You can make a "good" model with any set of data. It's really easy to put a model together that's garbage. The mechanics of getting data into the right format and training a model with the latest libraries are very easy. But the validation part is where you need people who know what they're doing. That's very different than the data engineering part and serving the model. The coordination of all of this stuff is really the challenge in doing this at scale. People get computer science degrees to understand distributed systems and stuff. You probably aren't going to get that from your typical data science background. The differentiation of roles is one of the big changes that's come about to address this.

The other thing I've seen change is that people are thinking more about diversity, equity, and inclusion (DEI). I think that DEI is really hard, but the thing that's nice is that some aspects of it can be "productionized" away. By building processes in that create more equitable hiring decisions, you don't have to think about it that hard. The parts that do need mental energy to overcome your implicit bias, you can focus on. I think that this has been a good thing, but different companies are at different stages with this and I think it's a journey. It's sort of like a lifestyle change versus a diet.

The other change is how boot camps are viewed. Since data science is much more common, there are now tons of boot camps with varying business models.

Roy: Do you think the perception of boot camps has improved or worsened?

Julie: I think some have stood the test of time. Not naming names, but others have reputations as not so great.

Roy: Do you have any thoughts about degrees? We're starting to see more and more data science degrees, including bachelor's degrees in data science.

Julie: I'm torn on it. I'm not convinced that a bachelor's in data science makes a ton of sense, knowing a bunch of techniques, but no real in-depth experience in a domain. My bias here is that I did a PhD and decided I didn't want to stay in it and then switched over to data science. One of the reasons I liked that path is that I learned something really cool. I can tell you about the chemical evolution of the galaxy and it's a fun story. But I also had to learn how to think. It depends on what these programs are like, but needing to go into a business situation is just different than anything you'll get in a classroom. So having and internship or a practicum is something that I think is critical. As an undergrad, you're not going to learn how to think on your own. The height of your achievement is doing problem sets, which is not the same as facing the kind of ambiguity that you'll have to deal with as a data scientist. Not that problem sets aren't important. I married someone I did problem sets with!

Even in the past couple of years these programs have changed. Also as data position titles have changed, I don't necessarily know what the title means. We've struggled with what to title different roles.

As Mozilla's CFO has related to us a bunch, you're being handed a gift - you're being handed someone's career for the next few years. It starts with sourcing and how you write the job rec. What kind of possibilities are you opening for people? Making life more difficult based on titles is something that you have to be really careful about.

Roy: In this book, one of the points I am trying to make is that you really need to understand what the role is so that you can describe it as clearly as possible. You don't want candidates to be surprised. Don't just throw in every buzzword you can think of. I think that titles are even trickier. It can be very political or constrained by other things within the company.

Julie: All of this stuff is hard. I'd like to have the attitude of "titles don't matter" and for things to be a meritocracy, but that's not how it works.

I think about this a lot in terms of career potential. I could promote someone to a higher level, with a title like "principal data scientist", but what will that mean for their next job at another company? Will it look like title inflation or be strange if their next title has a lower sounding level?

At Mozilla we put together a career level guide. The intent wasn't only to make career choices at Mozilla, but also how to make this applicable to the larger arc of their career.

On the other hand places with no titles have problems. They pretend it's a meritocracy, but it's not. You'll see people who were doing director level stuff, but then in their next job they are stuck with the title "software engineer" or something. This disproportionally effects folks from minoritized backgrounds, so it ends up being a DEI issue. It's kind of the hiring equivalent of "I don't see color".

Roy: It's definitely hard. How do you do things in a way that are fair, motivating, set people up for later success, but also doesn't shoot yourself in the foot? You could promote everyone in the company, for example, but then those people have nowhere to go within the company.

Julie: I'll let you know when I have it all figured out!

I think there are multiple things. One is operating under transparency. Having things as standard processes. From a legal perspective it acts as a CYA[11] effect. Having a standard process is the easiest way for things to be more equitable and explainable. Even if you end up changing things later, you at least understand how you got there and can explain how decisions were made. Having a robust process for hiring and promotions helps even past hiring.

Roy: What are your thoughts on how to make hiring decisions and making the process fair?

---

[11]"Cover your ass"

Julie: I've been on panels where you get a scoring rubric for each interview question and the interviews are paired, so there are always two interviewers. The questions are scored independently and then everyone gets to vote and then you discuss why you voted the way you did and then the hiring manager makes the decision based on all of that input.

But even before hiring begins, you need to work on your culture to make sure people want to come and importantly create an environment that would make them want to stay.

Roy: What else do you spend your time on related to hiring and what else do you think people should focus on to improve their hiring?

Julie: My not-so-hot take is that in order to hire well you need to put in a *lot* of effort. You may need to work to overhaul your process. I've seen this when I had the chance at Twitter to build a team from scratch, I was able to build out one of the strongest, most diverse teams in the company. It starts with how you write your job rec and sourcing candidates.

My first job as a manager is to make sure that my team is "good": good emotionally, good technically, good at communication. Being engaged in the hiring process is a big part of that. Every time you add a person, you have a new team. It's a constant state of evolution and a bad hire can be poison. If you make a hiring mistake, it's costly and painful for everyone involved, including the mishire.

Roy: How do you make sure that you get team buy-in on new hires?

Julie: It depends on the role. While I was at Twitter I would try to make sure that there was someone from my team in all of the interviewing pairs. Typically the team was well aligned because we created the job rec together. I also try to be as transparent as possible.

At first I wanted everyone to have input, but eventually there were too many people on the team for that to be practical. At the end of the day, as a manager, you need to own the decision and take responsibility for any less than ideal outcomes. That's part of putting your reports first.

Roy: Thanks so much for talking with me and lending your perspective. How can people follow you online?

Julie: Thanks for having me. People can find me at @jkru[12] on Twitter.

---

[12]https://twitter.com/jkru

Chapter 3: Determining what roles you need

$$\nabla_x C = (W^1)^T \cdot (f^1)' \cdot \ldots \cdot (W^{L-1})^T \cdot (f^{L-1})' \cdot (W^L)^T \cdot (f^L)' \cdot \nabla_{a^L} C$$

One of the most import parts about hiring is really understanding what you're trying to accomplish and who can help you accomplish it. In this chapter we will consider if and how data science and machine learning make sense for your business goals, specifically laying out what needs to be done and matching that up with the most relevant skill set, team structure, and titles for those roles.

Defining your business goal

While this book is about hiring data science and machine learning practitioners, it's important to start by looking at the big picture of what you are trying to achieve in order to determine what you're hiring needs truly are. Data science and machine learning are methods and technologies that have generated a lot of hope and hype. Like other technologies that have emerged over the years, people are eager to apply them, sometimes without fully understanding what they are or their true utility. To start your hiring process you need to clearly define what you are trying to achieve from a business perspective and then understand how data science and machine learning fit into that vision. Once you've established your business needs, you can then determine what new roles you need to best achieve your business goals.

Your specific business goal will be the most important thing in determining who you need to hire. Some organizations are at the very start of their journey and need to hire someone who can act as a data science jack-of-all-trades to kickstart their data science capability. Others have a mature organization and simply need to hire an additional role player for their team. Most organizations will be somewhere in between, building out from the small start they already have. All of this will ultimately stem from your business goal. The better defined that is, the better chance you have of hiring success.

You would not be reading this book if you didn't think that your business goals required data science or machine learning capability. Nonetheless, it's good to explicitly lay out the goals to clearly define those needs. Additionally, you want to estimate the value and feasibility of your business goal. The best case scenario is of course to have a both a highly valuable and highly feasible business goal. The value will depend on several factors specific to your business. Ideally the value can be expressed in concrete monetary terms, but this is typically difficult to estimate, beyond a loose range. The feasibility also relies on many factors specific to your business. This chapter will hopefully give you a better idea of whether data science and machine learning are reasonable approaches to your problem, but you may be in a chicken and egg scenario, where not having existing DS and ML capability may mean that you cannot make a well informed estimate of the feasibility. In that case, a consultation with an external data scientist may be a worthwhile investment.

How do data science and machine learning fit in?

With your high level business goal identified, it's important to then understand if and how data science and machine learning are appropriate for addressing the problems you need to solve to achieve that goal.

Why would you need data science or machine learning?

Data science and machine learning can help address a very wide variety of business problems. Some typical scenarios when an organization might need data science or machine learning include:

- You need to make accurate predictions beyond the capability of intuition
  - E.g. demand forecasting, asset pricing, arrival time estimation, anomaly detection, etc
- You need to scale a process that is inefficient or impossible with humans
  - E.g. product recommendations, triaging customer support, search, image recognition
- You need to extract insights and trends from data you have or could collect
  - E.g. understanding the seasonality of your product demand

Equally important is that you can spell out how the capability would affect decisions in the company or improve your product, and estimate how it would ultimately affect your organization's bottom line.

Why would you *not* need data science or machine learning?

Although the reasons you would not need these capabilities are essentially the opposite of why you would need them, it's sometimes useful to explicitly spell out the reasons when trying to determine your need. It's common for organizations to adopt new technologies and methodologies like DS and ML as they start to gain popularity (i.e. hype), but that does not necessarily mean that your organization needs (or is ready) for them.

You shouldn't pursue DS or ML solutions:

- Just because an investor/customer/journalist/random inter-net person thinks you should.
- If you have no data yet.
- If you don't have some data infrastructure in place yet.
- You can't think of specific use cases and the magnitude of the effect they'd have on your bottom line.
- You're only in it for the marketing value[13].

If your organization is in the fortunate position to pursue R&D with less concern for financial return, you may be able to adopt some of these approaches before they would make sense for other organizations.

When can you move forward with data science and machine learning

Besides having explicitly identified goals that match up with DS and ML solutions, it's important to recognize whether you're ready to implement those solutions yet.

As the data scientist Monica Rogati has observed, "first you need to be able to count"[14]. While this may sound glib, it means that you first need basic data related capabilities in your organization before you can pursue more complex and advanced techniques, such as ML. You must first have the basic infrastructure in place to collect and handle data. This does not necessarily mean the infrastructure to develop and deploy DS and ML solutions, but rather the more foundational data infrastructure that will allow the initial steps to

---

[13]Undoubtedly some marketers will disagree with this opinion.

[14]The AI Hierarchy of Needs, Monica Rogati

access and explore your data and begin working on proof of concept level analysis and ML. Additionally, you should have basic metrics in place to begin to be able to understand your baseline capabilities and how improvements in performance would translate into ROI for your DS and ML efforts.

Defining the roles you need

As was illustrated in previous chapters, you need to understand where in the multi-dimensional data science spectrum your needs lie. Do you need someone who whose primary purpose is around reporting? Do you need someone who's primary duties will lie around maintaining production machine learning models? Do you need someone who will focus on statistical experiments to understand your product's users and features?

Once you have identified your specific business need for data science or machine learning capability, it's important to distill that need into specific roles. The breadth of data science and machine learning engineering roles means that this may require more effort than what you might expect at first glance. You need to decide what type of role you need and how that role will fit into your existing or planned team.

The many roles in data science

As previously mentioned in chapter 2, the tasks that data scientists may be responsible for is very large. Those tasks can include:

- Finding and collecting data
- Cleaning data
- Exploring data

- Building data transformation pipelines
- Formulating metrics
- Creating reports
- Creating dashboards
- Designing and interpreting experiments
- Developing predictive models, e.g. machine learning models
- Deploying predictive models
- Maintaining predictive models
- Creating web apps and APIs
- Choosing services and tools to accomplish any of the above
- Communicating with stakeholders (internal or external)
- Fixing problems in any of the above

Examples of project-specific tasks

A dashboarding project might break down like this:

- The raw data needs to be tracked down and permission to access it needs to be granted.
- The raw data needs to be explored and discussed with stakeholders.
- Data transforms need to be finalized and cleaned data made available in a data warehouse or similar and recurring jobs deployed.
- The frontend and backend of the dashboard need to be designed and written.
- The dashboard needs to be deployed and secured.
- The pipeline and dashboard needs to be maintained.

A machine learning component of a product might breakdown like this:

- Performance metrics need to be created.
- Training data needs to be collected and labelled, if necessary.

- The machine learning model needs to be developed.
- Data cleaning, transformations, and feature creation pipelines need to be finalized and deployed, with clean features available in a data warehouse or similar.
- The model and pipelines need to be QA'd.
- The model needs to be deployed.
- Data capture to track model performance needs to be built and deployed.
- Model performance and feature health needs to be monitored.
- The pipelines and model need to be maintained.

Who is responsible for these tasks in different organizations can vary greatly. In a small startup or a new data science organization within a company, these tasks may all be handled by single generalist data scientist. Typically having a single person to cover all of those tasks is a very temporary situation. The people who can do all of those things well are incredibly difficult to find, so-called unicorns, and even when you can find such a person their ability will not scale to multiple projects. Ultimately you will need a data science or machine learning team.

The universe of data science roles in 2021

Over the past decade the titles and roles of data scientists have evolved. The generalist "data scientist" still exists, but many other titles and roles have also emerged, some existing since before "data science" became a common term. Roles and titles that currently exist include:

- Generalist data scientist
- Data analyst
- The experimenter or A/B tester

- Product analyst
- ML engineer
- Data engineer (with many sub-roles)
- The dashboard specialist
- MLOps engineer
- Analytics engineer
- ML researcher
- ML modeler
- ML developer
- Full-stack MLE
- DS manager
- The DS exec
- Operations research engineer
- Decision scientist

As you can see there are many roles and titles in use. The exact nature and scope of these roles and titles is highly dependent on the organization. How these fit in your organization will depend on both your specific need and potentially on what titles have already been established.

Determining the roles you need

To help you determine which roles you need, you need to consider which specific tasks you need to accomplish and which skills are needed to accomplish them. Additionally, you need to consider what capabilities already exist in your organization and any concrete plans you have for future growth. If, for example, you are starting a new team which you intend to grow, you may want to hire someone who can do both technical work and team management.

> # A key takeaway
>
> Because of the growing number of titles and roles related to data science and the ambiguity around what each role does, the single most important thing you can do is to crisply describe the role that you need to hire for.

Let's consider a few different scenarios.

Scenario I: A blank-slate proof of concept

Many companies want to start making better use of data and get the benefit of the latest technologies (i.e. data science and machine learning). These companies may want to start with the smallest possible team on a few proof-of-concept (PoC) projects. In this case a single generalist data scientist is likely the best choice. To successfully develop and implement these PoC's, the DS will need a wide range of skills, likely including data engineering, software development, server management, strong communication skills, and project management skills. Most crucial will be a hacker[15] mindset to work around issues that will arise on (necessarily) under-supported projects.

Depending on the specific situation, hiring a consultant or a full-time generalist DS are likely both good option in this scenario.

Scenario II: Productionizing or scaling a prototype

If you have a completed proof of concept that has met the criteria for initial success, the next step is often putting that model or system into production or scaling up it from a single instance or use

---

[15]Here I'm using *hacker* in the sense of a programmer who can make do with available resources to solve problems, rather than *hacker* in the sense of someone who subverts computer security.

case. In this scenario, you are likely crossing into more engineering heavy territory. While creating the PoC may have focussed on getting access to the data, exploring the data, calculating KPI's[16] or creating features useful for ML, and creating and deploying a basic dashboard, webapp, or API, the next stage typically means productionizing in a more robust way. You are likely looking at issues related to model or dashboard deployment in a repeatable and revokable way, building robust data pipelines, monitoring the system's status and predictive performance, and iterating the underlying analytics. This means that you need a team with experience around software and system development, data engineering, and model and application devops. Members of this team may consist of more experienced generalist DS's, but likely you want to look for MLE's, data engineers, and software engineers with experience in systems design, potentially front/backend web dev, and devops. In practice it is common for data scientists to start down the path of MLE, data engineering, or MLOps when they are faced with learning the skills to perform these tasks, often learning best practices from software engineers.

In this scenario, it's important to look at your existing capabilities outside of strictly DS or ML to understand which additional roles you may need to hire. It may make more sense to assemble a team of existing people within the broader organization, or you may need to hire for those additional skills needed to productionize and / or scale your existing early-stage solution.

Scenario III: Adding an additional role player

If your data science organization is mature, it's likely that you will be hiring for additional role players. Depending on the specifics of the business, this could be a generalist, but is more likely a more specialized role, such as an MLE who focuses on ML training infrastructure, rather than someone who needs to work end-to-end

---

[16]Key performance indicator

on deployment efforts. In this case it is important to understand the specific needs at that time and those that are likely to arise in the medium to long term. Do you need skills you currently don't have on your team? Do you need a senior person? Do you have the resources to train a more junior person? While these are often questions that are difficult to answer with high confidence, this is typically an easier scenario than trying to build our a less mature organization.

The skills you need to hire for follow from the tasks you need to complete

To understand the roles you need to hire, you first need to understand what skills your team needs. To understand what skills are needed, you need to understand what tasks are needed to accomplish your organization's business goals. In this section I will lay out some of the common tasks that data scientists and machine learning engineers need to perform and the associated skills needed to complete those tasks. Understanding the tasks and skills needed to accomplish your organization's goals will allow you to better identify the best candidates, starting by describing the specific role well.

The subject matter expert vs the data science generalist

Often employers are faced with the question of whether they should hire someone who is more familiar with their specific domain, but weak in data science and machine learning, or someone who is strong in data science and machine learning, but unfamiliar with the specific domain.

Ideally, you'd hire someone who is an expert at both, but that is usually not feasible, as the two skill sets are often very different[a]. Where on the spectrum of subject matter expert to data science expert to hire is a very difficult question to answer. Another way to think about the question is how the *team* working on the problems covers both subject matter and DS/ML. That means that you may need to have separate people who work together on the team. Their combined knowledge can cover both the domain and the DS/ML techniques.

In teams I've worked on, we've had success hiring data scientists and machine learning engineers with at least some base of knowledge in the areas of interest, even if they were not experts. For example, a person with a background in mechanical engineering, who has been working in DS/ML, will usually be able to quickly get up to speed on many types of physical engineering systems, working with a subject matter expert stakeholder or team mate.

---

[a]This is rapidly changing, as data science and machine learning techniques are being integrated into more and more fields, often in educational settings.

Examples of task to skills translations

Let's take a look at some specific tasks, constituent sub-tasks, and the skills likely needed to complete those tasks. First we will take a look at data collection.

Task: Finding and collecting data

Collecting	Storing	Automating
Accessing and querying databases	Setting up databases	Scripting data collection
Using web API's	Using cloud-based storage	Using cloud-based workers
Scraping the web		

Then looking at the first sub-task, "accessing and querying databases", the corresponding skills are likely

Skills: **Accessing and querying databases**

Knowledge of SQL	Experience querying document stores	Experience querying key-value stores
Experience querying graph databases	Experience with SQL clients	Experience with DB specific API libraries

As a second example, lets look at the task of deploying predictive models (e.g. machine learning models).

Task: **Deploying predictive models**

Building data pipelines	Setting up data / feature stores	Designing a useful API
Packaging and deploying the model	Deploying and/or integrating serving infrastructure	

And looking at the sub-task of "packaging and deploying the model" and the common skills needed to accomplish that.

Skills: **Packaging and deploying the model**

Refactoring the code into a package or module	Determining minimal runtime environment and dependencies	Experience creating runtime environments (e.g. docker containers)

Skills: Packaging and deploying the model

Experience using cloud based runtime environment orchestration tools or services (e.g. [hosted] Kubernetes)	Experience with cloud-based ML platforms	Experience creating integration tests

Translating from tasks to skills

To understand the skills that your team members need to success-fully complete the tasks they are faced with, you need to translate from the specific tasks to the broader set of general and specific skills. Once again, we remind ourselves that data science is very broad and by digging deep into these tasks and the associated skills, we might be able to focus in on the most appropriate set of skills.

In the last section we saw a couple of examples of how you might go from a given task to a set of specific skills. There are a lot of skills that a data scientist or MLE might potentially have[17]. The goal is to understand which skills are the most relevant for the tasks that a new team member will most likely need to accomplish. To do that, you can use the skills tables in Appendix I to translate from expected tasks to likely skills.

Unfortunately these skills tables will not tell you which skills are the most valuable for your organization, as that depends largely on the goals, current infrastructure, team, and level of DS/ML maturity in the organization. Hopefully working through the tables will give you a much clearer picture of which skill sets are most likely to be valuable.

[17]See Appendix I for a more complete listing of tasks and corresponding skills, which is simply too large to include here.

Training versus hiring

A common question is whether it's more practical to train existing employees as data scientists or machine learning practioners rather than hiring new, experienced people.

The likelihood of success will depend largely on the situation. You are more likely to have success if you:

- Have in-house DS/ML experts that can serve as teachers and guides.
- Have strong executive level support.
- Are training current employees with adjacent skill sets (e.g. programming or basic data analysis)
- Have support for the tools, access, and infrastructure needed.

Under the right circumstances this can be done well, but that's not often the case.

You are less likely to have success if you:

- Have no existing in-house experts to double check things.
- Lack the support and infrastructure.
- Are doing this purely for cost-saving reasons.

Having an employee bootstrap themself into DS/MLE knowledge is equivalent to hiring a non-experienced DS/MLE without anyone to mentor or guide them. It's not a guaranteed failure, but makes success difficult.

The roles you need to hire for follow from the task-related skills

Once you have understood the skill sets needed on your team, you can best understand which roles your team needs. Often this will be no great surprise, but you will hopefully have more clarity than you started out with. Other times you may realize that you in fact need to hire for a role than is different than what you were expecting, and possibly a completely new role to you team, such as an MLE or analytics engineer.

It's also possible that you will need to hire for a role that does not cleanly fit into the established roles in the marketplace (ref. "data scientist" in 2009). In this case you will be better equipped to describe the specific tasks and skills that will be associated with this role.

Examples of skill sets for specific roles

Role: Data analyst

Knowledge of SQL	Exploratory data analysis	Data visualization
Complex data filtering	Understanding statistical concepts	Basic statistical modeling
Building dashboards	Communicating results	

Role: ML modeler

Knowledge of SQL	Exploratory data analysis	Data visualization
Programming in Python or R	Knowledge of traditional and contemporary ML techniques	Model performance metric creation
Training, assessing, and iterating models	Feature creation and architecture selection	Communicating results

The example skill sets above are by no means exhaustive. See Appendix II for a more complete listing of skills by role.

Translating from tasks and skills to roles

For your new role, you ultimately need to hire someone who can satisfactorily perform the required tasks. Typically the tasks define the role more than the skills, but the skills are what you need to assess when hiring. Because of that, you need to understand both the relevant tasks and the requisite skills to define the role well.

Appendix II contains a more exhaustive list of roles and the skills those roles commonly have or require. Once you have identified the skills that are likely necessary to perform the tasks that your team needs, you can then decide which type of role best matches that need.

As previously mentioned, your need may not cleanly match an common industry role. It's best to think of the roles, as laid out in Appendix II, as a starting point. The description you use for your role may be as simple as "MLE", or may need a descriptive modifier like "ML Infrastructure Engineer". Additionally, for strategic reasons, you may want to hire for a more general role than your current specific set of tasks. In that case you may want to intentionally advertise for a more generic role.

Determining job titles for new roles

Determining titles is one of the trickier requirements when hiring for a new role. You would like to create a job title that is simultaneously descriptive, fits with the established conventions of the organization, and is not unnecessarily limiting for the person in the role. As with many other aspects in hiring, the relative newness, breadth, and ambiguity of data science can cause difficulties.

Naming can be tricky

One customer whom I worked with in the past was interested in hiring for the role of data engineer, but faced a peculiar problem. Their company was a traditional industrial company that employed many "physical" engineers (e.g. mechanical, chemical, civil, etc engineers). Existing company rules stated that an employee could only have the word "engineer" in their job title if they had completed an engineering degree. This was obviously a development that happened in isolation from the evolution of titles in the world of computing. This scenario put the hiring manager at a disadvantage, as they were unable to advertise the role with a name that would attract the applicant pool that they were seeking. Ultimately they went with a compromise title of "data engineering developer".

Building on the roles landed on in the last section, ultimately following from your business goals, tasks to accomplish those goals, and skills needed to successfully complete those tasks, appropriate titles can be chosen. For many it will be as straight-forward as using the name of that role as the job title. For others, they will be bound by the existing title conventions or may want to strategically choose a broader title (e.g. simply "data scientist") to enable flexibility or for other reasons. If possible, go with the title that is the most descriptive, but still broad enough to allow for some lateral expansion of duties.

Do titles matter?

One of the perennial debates that you can watch online is over the importance of job titles. I am going to solve the issue once and for all.

Just kidding.

One line of argument is that titles shouldn't matter because of the fluid nature of the work done at tech companies (especially early-stage companies). Dispensing with titles removes barriers in communication or getting work done, or so the argument goes. One the other end of the spectrum is the idea that very specific, graded titles (think the military as the canonical example) allows people in the org to easily understand what people's responsibilities, likely skills, and path for advancement are. There are many variations between these ends of the spectrum, such as allowing different internal and external facing titles.

Both of these approaches offer advantages and some clear disadvantages. What makes the most sense for your org is beyond the scope of this book. So, no, I didn't solve this debate.

Wrapping up: Roles

Ultimately the roles you need to hire for depend on what (business) problems you need to solve. While this feels obvious, it's helpful to take a step back and think about those needs to land on the most specific description possible of the role you need to hire.

Because data science is so broad and roles and titles are often vague, it is easy for there to be a mismatch between the expectations of the hiring manager and job candidates. The best strategy to get the most suitable applicant pool is to be able to describe the tasks and skills related to the role as accurately as possible.

Unless you are at a company with a strategy of hiring lots of generalists and then repurposing them for whatever tasks are at hand (typically very large companies), it's probably best to work through the catalogue of tasks, skills, and roles, to most precisely identify the roles you need to hire for.

Interview: Chris Albon, Wikimedia

Chris Albon is the Director of Machine Learning at Wikimedia (the foundation behind Wikipedia). He previously ran data science at Devoted as well as several non-profits and startups. Prior to working in data science, Chris completed a PhD in quantitative political science.

Chris is the author of Machine Learning with Python Cookbook[a] and the creator of Machine Learning Flashcards[b]. He can be found online at chrisalbon.com[c] and @chrisalbon[d] on Twitter.

In the interview below, Chris discusses some of the main challenges faced by machine learning hiring managers and some of the approaches that he has used to address those challenges.

---

[a]https://www.oreilly.com/library/view/machine-learning-with/9781491989371/
[b]https://machinelearningflashcards.com/
[c]https://chrisalbon.com/
[d]https://twitter.com/chrisalbon

Roy: Let's start off by having you tell us some about your background and current role.

Chris: My name is Chris. I am currently the Director of Machine Learning at Wikimedia, which is the non-profit foundation that hosts Wikipedia. My background is coming into tech from a more humanitarian background. I have a quantitative background that led to joining some non-profits, founding my own company, joining some other startups, and then joining another non-profit, the Wikimedia Foundation. I have some unique experience around international teams, remote work, and developing culture in companies where people may only see each other once or twice a year and come from really different geographical backgrounds. Dealing with different timezones and async stuff is something that has followed me throughout a lot of my career. At Ushahidi, a Kenyan non-profit, we had folks all around the world, at FrontlineSMS, where I had my first DS role, at my own startup, and now at The Wikimedia Foundation, where I'm building out a machine learning team. We have folks everywhere from Switzerland, Uganda, to San Francisco.

Roy: What are the roles that you've hired for in that time?

Chris: I have hired everything from data engineering roles, data science / analytics roles, machine learning roles, and the most recent one, which I'm hiring for right now, is an SRE[18] role. I've never actually hired for that before, but I've done a wide variety of hiring in a lot of different spaces around data.

I think the role that I'm best suited to hire for is machine learning roles. That's the place that I feel like I can contribute my own knowledge most to the interview process.

Roy: Given that experience, what do see as the biggest challenges in hiring data scientists and machine learning engineers?

Chris: I think it probably depends most on the seniority. So if you're hiring a junior person, the hardest thing is that a lot of them look very similar on paper. For example, this one has a boot camp and this one did a master's program, but none of them have job experience. They may have side projects, but they're often like other side projects, like ones that we've all done.

I think one of the differences is that when you and I were getting started[19] if you did anything with data it was crazy. If you took some crime data and did some analysis people were like, "whoa, no one's

---

[18]Site reliability engineer
[19]Roy's note: A long, long time ago...

ever seen that before!" These days every single one of these boot camps is having the students grind out these analyses in Jupyter notebooks and it's hard for the candidates to stand out. On my end it's hard for me to filter candidates. You can have ten candidates and see that they're all different, but you can't tell which ones really hit the spot.

Roy: Some of these programs are so big, that when you get an applicant pool you'll notice the same projects over and over.

Chris: Yeah.

I think the other hard thing is probably that a lot of the folks on the junior level come in from science and almost all of them approach things from the perspective of science. They'll have some really complex algorithm that they're using to look at housing data in Boston or they're using deep learning to figure out that kind of stuff. But a lot of the work of a day-to-day MLE or data scientist is around putting things in production, or managing things, or scaling things, or figuring out how to grab stuff off of ten different databases and clean it and put it somewhere. That's the kind of stuff I'm really looking for. A lot of the boot camps and tutorials, many of which I've written, are really focused on the fun, sciency part. "This is this really interesting genetic algorithm that does that thing!" Whereas the bread and butter, which you'll actually be doing when you're a junior person coming on to the team, is actually not seen in their resume. As the hiring manager, I have a hard time distinguishing which one of these candidates I could add to a team that's building out a new data pipeline, who could contribute to that. It's difficult.

As they get more senior, people start to have more specialized skills and more specialized experiences. "Oh, I worked for five years on Kubernetes." And you're like, "Great! I need someone with Kubernetes experience. You're awesome!" That makes things a lot easier, which doesn't typically happen with more junior people.

With senior roles there are two kinds of issues that are pretty hard. One is their career direction. You'll see that because data science is so broad, that you can be looking at someone and be really interested in them, because you think they would be a great person to be, for example, "70% data scientist and 30% data engineer", but in reality, they see their focus as swapped. They want something different. So you can hire someone and then when they come onto the team, they feel that they are not doing what they want to be doing. I don't think there are enough titles and subdivision of titles in data science to really make it clear for many of the job posts that I write. Someone might feel that they are "48% this and 28% operations research and 10% whatever". Every candidate is some unique mix.

Roy: I've seen something similar from the hiring side. Sometimes people will refer candidates to you and realize that because data science and machine learning is so broad and vague, that people will project what they imagine the role to be. It makes it that much harder to find people and that much more important to try to be as crisp as possible in communicating what your company needs, even if the title on its own can't really communicate that.

Chris: If you don't have the job description crisp, which is really hard to do, particularly if there are other stakeholders involved with making that job description, you end up wasting a lot of time. You end up talking to people who were never interested in the job. This is part of the reason why my first conversation with every candidate is basically "my goal in this entire 20 minute call is either that we decide you should move on to the next step or we collectively decide that isn't a role that you want to do". And that's fine. I just want to put that out like, "hey, it's OK for us to come to the conclusion in this call that you just wouldn't really want to do this role, even if I offered it to you". That's true in a lot of cases. I've had people turn down roles because of technology, like, for example PHP. And I was glad we talked about that up front. It probably saved us a lot of time.

There's lots of stuff around that. At Devoted I was hiring a lot of people to do analytics. A lot of SQL analytics with a little bit of

Python. There were folks coming in who would say, "oh, I saw the job description for a data scientist with a focus on analytics, but how much ML are you really doing?" And my response is "None. No ML." If you have to have those conversations in person, you're going to waste so much time. I don't have an assistant, so it takes me 20 minutes to arrange a phone call after a few emails back and forth and then do a 20 minute phone call. So that's 40 minutes. I don't want to waste other team members' time on top of that, so it's best to get to that point as quickly as possible. And the best way to get to that is with a really clear job description.

Roy: What process do you use or prefer for making hiring decisions?

Chris: This is something I learned a lot from DJ Patil, who's a noted data scientist. We would go into meetings with everyone who interviewed a candidate and we were going to discuss the hiring decision. There were two things that DJ did that I really appreciated, but I thought he was maddeningly wrong so many times. One was that it would never be a vote. Team members would give you advice and consent, but it was the hiring manager's choice. Of course the hiring manager is going to consider the consent, but the hiring manager is considering the team, not the individuals. So you might have five IC's on the panel, who think the candidate would be a great IC, but you don't necessarily want that. You're building a team, not just a collection of IC's. He was really big on that and I think I learned a lot from that.

The other thing, which I really "hated" him for, until I asked him why he did it, was that DJ would never, ever score someone in the mid range. If the score range was 0-5, he would always score a zero or a five. If everyone else was saying four, he would say zero. I got so angry with him a few times. "Why are you doing this?!?" And his answer was so perfect. He said, "I don't want you to just agree. I don't want it to be a 2.5 out of 5. I want people to feel that we absolutely must hire this person and that we'll do whatever possible to try to get them. Or let's just move on." He was forcing us to have extreme positions. If we didn't have them, he would. I appreciated that, because it forced people out of their bubble. If you give people a scale, people will sit in the middle. Everyone sits in the middle. It's just a natural place to be. To have someone come in and force you to decided and think, saying, "if this is a weak no, then I'm a zero". I really appreciated that. It was a well thought out strategy. I have now implemented this strategy. I'm now trying to make sure I'm hiring for the team as a whole and also trying to shake people's opinion, trying to see how strongly they believe something. Try to see how much they're willing to fight for some candidate.

Hiring is the most costly and most valuable weapon I have as a manager. I get X hires and those X hires will create a team. Who I hire will create the team's culture, the team's experience, the team's productivity, all of that. I also don't get a ton of hires. I don't have 20 hires a week. I can deploy a million times a week before I get another hire. So I want to be fast, but it's super valuable to get it right.

I think those two things have made me a better hiring manager. I make better hires, more interesting hires, and shake up the team a little bit more with experience we might not have and make them think a bit harder about what we want. I think overall that's gone pretty well.

Roy: In your time working as a data scientist and DS/ML hiring manager, what have you seen as the biggest changes?

Chris: Probably two things. First, one that we touched on before. My first experience in tech was actually in web development. It was long enough ago that you were called "web master". A company would usually have just one web master who did everything. They were the frontend, backend, everything team, that one web master. These days, of course, there is a plethora of skills: design, UX, frontend dev, backend of the frontend, optimization, all of that stuff. In data science what I see is this explosion of job titles that's starting to happen. Whereas a few years ago, I think both of us would be like, "whoa, we're both data scientists". Right? But now you're seeing, "actually, I'm a backend MLOps person" or "I'm a frontend ML integrator". That kind of stuff. I don't think the titles have really solidified.

I would love MLOps. That's the thing I'm essentially hiring for, but that's not really a title that exists. That's not in the drop down menu. But this explosion of titles will be so useful a few years down the line. We'll be able to filter down candidates a lot better. But right now it's like the messy wild west, where someone says, "my title is 'Data Scientist', but actually I'm doing backend Kubernetes optimization."

I think it's been especially confusing, because large data science hirers, like Facebook, use terms differently. At Facebook "data science" is not what other people would call data science. It's analytics.

Roy: I kind of blame them for some of the name shifting. In a negative way.

Chris: You can have candidates, who come in and say, "I'm a data scientist and what I do is A/B testing, analytics, and a lot of SQL." And then you have other people who say, "I don't do any of that. I actually do the 'science' side, like Bayesian work and that kind of stuff." And then you have other people who come in and say, "oh, I actually just do productized ML." And we're all sharing the same title!

The second change I've seen is that when data science started there was a lot of low hanging fruit to be taken. Like a quick bar chart could show something that could make the sales team do better. A lot of that has been commercialized. So, for example, a churn analysis could be one API query away or is a built-in feature of some BI app. That means the big wins tend to be larger experiments. Bigger models, etc. That requires not only the machine learning part, but also the operations part. How do we set up the servers? How do we make things at scale? That means that the data scientist who really knows random forests, for example, is interesting, but the person who sort of know random forests, but really knows how to do MLOps and that kind of stuff is very, very interesting, because we really need those people.

Roy: Thanks so much for your insights, Chris.

Chris: You're welcome. Please check out Wikipedia!

Chapter 4: Creating a hiring strategy

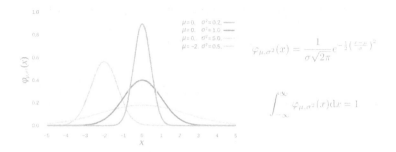

At this point you should have understood your organization's business problem, the tasks related to that problem, and ultimately landed on the role or roles that you need to fill. Now comes the time where you need to create a strategy for hiring that will get you where your organization needs to be, and hopefully in an efficient way.

At the highest level, you need to understand what problem you are trying solve and land on the best strategy for solving it. The problem faced by a hiring manager in a large tech company looking to add another data scientist to an already large team is very different than the problem faced by a startup founder looking to kickstart their ML efforts with their first data-related hire. Identifying your circumstances and crafting a strategy to match is the key to successful, efficient hiring.

In this chapter, I will walk you through many of the important considerations and decisions you need to make to create an effective hiring strategy. We will focus on two of the three main components of your hiring strategy: recruiting and structuring your process. Candidate assessment will be covered in Chapters 6 and 7. It's important to keep in mind that your hiring strategy is unlikely to be perfect from the beginning. You will need to adapt it to fix shortcomings as well as to adapt to the constantly changing hiring environment.

Determining your resources and constraints

An organization is really the people within it. When hiring, you are trying to find the next person who will help your organization meet its goals and contribute to making the organization even better. That said, you are largely at the mercy of your organization's resources and constraints. Given those, your hiring strategy and process should be seen as an optimization trying to best balance your hiring goals against those resources, and constraints.

If you could pay ten times the going market salary for a data scientist, you would have some great options. I'm guessing that you are not in a position to pay ten times the going rate and stay in business, though. Instead, you need to take stock of your resources and constraints, while also understanding the state of the market that you are operating in.

Resources

As a hiring manager, what resources are available to you? Of the following, which do you have access to?

- HR support for the hiring process, including sourcing candidates, screening resumes, and training interviewers.
- Applicant tracking software.
- Skills assessment software.

- A recruiting budget for job ads, attending job fairs, flying in candidates, branded schwag, etc.
- Experienced interviewers.
- The ability to pull in people from outside of your team / department.

At a large company with a large HR department, recruiting budget, and robust hiring process, these questions may be superfluous and you may need to simply make some small adaptations to the current process to hire data scientists and MLE's. In an early stage startup, on the other hand, you may have almost none of these and need to make due the best you can.

Constraints

Everyone would love to hire the *perfect* people for the job, but you are limited by the constraints you are operating in as a hiring manager. Besides a budget for compensating employees, you need to think about your time budget for yourself and other people that will be involved in the hiring process.

Questions to ask yourself:

- How much time can you spend on hiring for the currently needed role(s)?
- What is your budget for hiring related expenses?
- What is your hiring timeline?
- Can you support candidates that need work authorization?

Goals

Having identified the role(s) that you need to hire, your obvious goal is to hire the "best" person you can get for that role, but you may have other goals or requirements in hiring that extend beyond the intrinsic aspects of the tasks. You may be looking to hire a more diverse team of employees. You may need to find candidates with government security clearances or other specific credentials. Any of these will need to be taken into account in your strategy for recruiting and hiring.

Building a diverse team

In recent years there has been much more emphasis on creating more diverse[a] teams, especially at organizations in the US. As anyone who has embarked on trying to build a more diverse team knows, it can be difficult. The biggest question is how you attract and retain a more diverse team.

In the US there are laws[b] in place to prevent discrimination in hiring and other workplace activities based on legally protected classes. Under certain circumstances though, an employer *is* allowed to take those factors into account. You should make sure that your HR team has consulted with an employment attorney and has clear guidance on what is and is not allowed. A reasonable overview of the US federal rules can be found here[c].

What this means practically is that you need to focus on attracting and retaining applicants from the categories you are looking to increase on your team. Practical steps include:

- Sponsoring and attending events related to those categories.
- Advertising your roles on demographic specific forums.
- Reducing barriers, such as specific education requirements that may unnecessarily reduce your applicant pool size.
- Creating (and advertising) a fair hiring process (see Chapters 6 and 7).
- Making it clear in your job ads and related material that you support a diverse team.

- Offering strong benefits and a collegial environment that welcomes everyone.

What candidates tend to react negatively to are actions that seem artificial or performative. Is this just some corporate effort designed primarily for PR reasons or does it seem like the organization is really putting forth a genuine effort? The difference can be subtle and difficult to achieve.

[a]Here diversity refers to having people from different backgrounds and statuses across a number of dimensions, including race, ethnicity, gender, sexual orientation, physical ability, age, etc.

[b]It's very important to note here that I am not, in fact, a lawyer

[c]https://www.aclusocal.org/en/inclusion-targets-whats-legal

Understanding the job market

A major component in planning your hiring strategy is understanding the market. How many applicants should you expect? Do you need to actively recruit? Can you afford someone who can actually perform the needed work?

Data science and machine learning have been among the most hyped areas of technology in the past decade. As a result of that hype and market conditions for some groups of potential data scientists[20], the job market has become very saturated with candidates as of 2021. Early predictions in the era of data science were that the demand for people with data science skills would far outpace the supply of people with data science skills[21]. More recent studies[22] indicate that the number of data science job openings has

[20]A massive shortage in academic jobs has led many recent STEM PhD graduates to look for greener pastures and data science has been seen as one of the greenest.

[21]Most famously by a report put out in 2011 by McKinsey.

[22]See this piece on KDnuggets (2018) and this report from IBM (2017).

in fact been growing rapidly, but all evidence from those hiring indicate that the situation on the ground is effectively a market flooded with candidates.

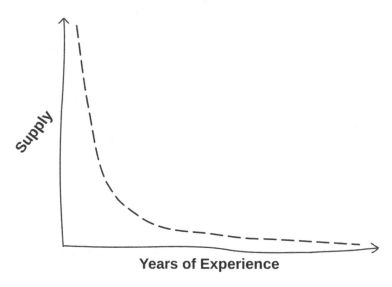

Supply of data science professionals versus years of experience

The relative newness and hype around data science and machine learning jobs has led to a power law like distribution in the supply of candidates versus their amount of experience. The proliferation of boot camps, online training courses, and master's degree programs has been a reaction to this explosively growing interest in joining the field. This has resulted in a huge number of people with the basic data science skills, but little hands-on experience, relative to the more seasoned practitioners. This means that those hiring for entry level or more junior level roles tend to face an overwhelming number of applications, while those hiring for the most senior level roles may have a hard time finding enough candidates. This has implications both for the required scalability of your hiring strategy and of course the relative salary demands.

Is there a data scientist bubble?

The question of whether the data science job market is a bubble comes up often online and has for the past several years. Given the current, apparently exponential growth in the supply of data scientists, there needs to continue to be an exponential growth in the number of new roles to prevent something like a bubble.

No one knows what will happen, but I think the most likely scenario is that there will not be a bubble burst, but rather a gradual market correction in supply versus demand. There are many factors that are likely to affect this:

- The "democratization" of data science via new, easy to use tools and the dissemination of techniques to non-specialists, leading to lower demand for dedicated data scientists.
- Organizations learning the hard way that hype-driven data initiatives tend to have poor ROI, leading to more conservative launching of new projects and slowing growth in demand for data scientists.
- The maturation of technologies and knowledge about how to apply data science. The low hanging fruit has mostly been picked and we're left with fewer, more "serious" tasks.

I am optimistic that most data scientists will be able to adapt to these changes, as that is already the nature of their jobs: learn, adapt, learn some more, adapt some more.

The Covid-19 pandemic and the emergence of remote work

Remote work has been steadily gaining momentum in recent years. The global pandemic due to Covid-19 has kicked the movement to remote work into extremely high gear. It's unclear what the long-term effect of the pandemic will be on in-person versus remote work (will we all go back to the office?), but it seems very likely that remote work will be much more common than it was before the pandemic, as people have better understood the possibilities.

Besides the incredibly rapid adoption of remote working out of necessity, the economic side effects of the pandemic led to massive layoffs at many companies. In this time, some also used it as a chance to transition their careers to data science and ML. This has made the market even more saturated with data science job seekers.

As hiring continues or picks back up from this downturn, organizations hiring will be faced with potentially much larger applicant pools, especially if they have decided to hire remote team members. This means that being prepared to scale your candidate assessment strategy will be all the more important.

The effects of this increased applicant pool and remote positions on compensation is yet to be seen, but may potentially depress salaries to some extent[23].

Scaling to meet your expected applicant volume

What does it mean to scale your hiring strategy? In 2015 I set about hiring at the early-stage startup that I had joined. At the time,

---

[23]There is speculation that the restart of activity after the pandemic will cause a hiring spike. How that plays out with a potentially increased applicant pool is unclear. This will probably be the thing in this book that ages least well. Hello from 2021! :)

the process I chose was in-depth and rather time consuming, but yielded a lot of information on candidates and gave them a strong flavor of the type of work our team was focused on. Skip forward just a couple years and I was at a new company and once again hiring to build a team. I decided to adopt a very similar process. What I was unaware of and unprepared for was the growth that had happened in the overall market in those couple of years. The process I had designed had handled a couple hundred applicants well, but could not handle 3 - 4 times that number in a reasonable way. I had to scramble to adapt the process as best as possible for that hiring round and then completely overhauled the process for the subsequent round of hiring, with scaling foremost in mind.

When you think about scaling, you need to think again about your resources and constraints. What is a realistic time budget to spend on hiring for yourself and others involved? How much HR support can you expect if you need it beyond whatever is standard? If you receive X applicants and have Y time to spend, will $Y \div X$ be enough time to process the applications in an effective way? How much time will you need to spend on recruiting before those applications are even in the system? Do you even have a system to accept applications?

Engineering hiring versus DS/ML hiring

In speaking with teammates from the engineering team in the same company, openings for DS-oriented roles tended to see 3 - 5 times as many applicants as software developer roles. While the hope is usually to aim for a level of consistency in the process for hiring technical roles, the differences in numbers of applicants can necessitate different processes or strategies. In my experience, which is clearly dependent on company size, etc, HR support was vital in certain aspects here, but it required a fair amount of education for HR to fully understand the different scales.

When thinking about how to allocate your time, a common approach is to structure your hiring process in such a way that the amount of time you spend at a certain stage is relative to the likelihood that you will make an offer to the candidate. That means that at the earliest stage of the process you will typically spend very little time on a given applicant, e.g. skimming a resume, whereas you might spend hours with a single candidate in the final stages of the process. This is a key component of scaling and we will discuss it more below when we talk about how to structure your hiring process.

Determining your recruiting strategy

As described previously, when hiring data scientists and machine learning engineers, the problem is often less "finding data scientists is hard", but more often "finding the people you want is hard". Two general strategies for finding the people you want are:

1. Casting a wide net and sorting through a very large number of applicants.
2. Specifically targeting people that you think would likely be good matches.

Typically people choose to do a combination of the two, sometimes with (partially) parallel tracks in their assessment and interviewing process.

In this section we will touch on some of the general steps in recruiting for both of those strategies.

What does it take to source high quality applicants?

Filling your hiring funnel with candidates is largely dependent on the reputation of your organization, market conditions, and active outreach.

In 2021 you are likely to have no problem filling your hiring funnel. The market is more in favor of employers than in previous years (though salaries are still very high) due to large scale layoffs during the Covid-19 pandemic. If you are looking for junior applicants, the challenges will be about attracting the highest quality junior candidates and filtering your funnel.

Attracting strong candidates is primarily about building a strong brand. This can be about your product brand if you are selling a consumer product. It can also be about your brand as an employer. Prospective employees tend to see the reputation of a company as a employer based on:

- Compensation (including salary, equity, and benefits)
- How well employees are treated and the overall environment
- How exciting the products and technologies are
- Health of the company as a business
- Strength of the team
- Having a positive impact on the world (or similar)

Different candidates will weigh all of these differently. Clearly, many of these aspects are part of the long-term arc of the organization and not something that most managers can directly influence in a substantive way. That said, you should of course strive to be part of what makes all of those aspects as positive as possible.

While those aspects of reputation may seem impossible to affect, you should look at what you can most directly affect and focus your effort there. At a smaller company the primary thing to focus on is evangelizing to people who are unfamiliar with it. At a larger organization, it may be the story you can tell about your specific team or sub-organization. What can you do to make your team as attractive as possible to prospective hires? Usually the answer comes down to the things you should be doing to ensure that your team is both well functioning and happy. This typically means insuring that your team has autonomy, support for technical and career growth, and a sense of psychological safety. I will discuss some more on this topic in Chapter 8 about setting your new hires up for success.

Active outreach

Along with brand building, which tends to be a long-term focused activity, the other main recruiting activity is active outreach, which I use in a broad sense to include activities such as cold contacting people, job fairs, and referral programs.

As with every other decision you make in creating your hiring strategy, you need to keep in mind your goals, resources, and constraints when deciding how to spend your resources on active outreach. It is easy to spend your time, money, and effort on busy, but relatively low-yield activities.

A quick run-down of activities follows:

Cold contacting potential candidates:

- Good for targeting specific, qualified-on-paper candidates, especially to help increase the portion of specific demographics that you're trying to go after.
- Potentially a high return activity if you have a strong brand and/or present a well targeted, genuine message.
- This can be very time consuming and potentially requires some cost to get access to people's inboxes (e.g. a recruiter level subscription to some services).

- Candidates can be easily turned off by generic, corny, or mis-targeted recruiting messages.
- Third party recruiters typically have a very loose grasp at best on what your team and company is like, which is very often detrimental.

Job fairs:

- Probably best for recruiting interns and new graduates from universities, as well as growing generic brand awareness growth.
- Time and sometimes money consuming.
- Typically require planning far in advance of the actual event.
- University job fairs are unlikely to be a source of experienced candidates (with the exception of those that include alumni).
- Consider sponsoring on-campus events outside of university job fairs if your are looking to hire students. These can be more expensive, but allow you to stand out instead of being just another name on a booth at the job fair.

Meetups, hackathons, and happy hours:

- These events can help spread awareness of your company and give you a forum for presenting more specifics about your company or team.
- Can involve a lot of resources and time.
- May or may not attract the candidates you want.

Referral programs:

- These can be cheaper than other recruiting activities.
- Your employees may be able to give potential candidates the best insight into what working in your organization is like.

- Because of the broad and vague nature of data science, employees outside of your team or department may have a poor understanding of the skills you are looking for and/or the relative skill level of the person they are referring.

Once again, with all of these activities, it's important to have as clear as possible of an understanding of what the roles you need to hire are. An email to a potential candidate with a clear, concise description of the role is much more likely to generate a positive response (unless you already have a very strong brand). When talking to potential candidates at a recruiting event, being able to accurately and thoughtfully describe the work done by the team, the open roles, and company life goes a very long way. In Chapter 5 we will spend more time on writing job descriptions, which is closely related to this.

Structuring your hiring process

Once you have a clear understanding of your goals, resources, constraints, and the state of the market, you need to structure your hiring process. Like several of the other topics discussed in this chapter, this will depend a lot on the size and structure of your organization. You may have very little room for customizing your process to meet your needs in a large, highly bureaucratic organization, or you may be starting from scratch in an early startup. In this section, I will assume that you are building from the ground up, but if not you should pay attention to parts that you might be able to shape to your needs.

Simply put, you want structure your process in such a way as to maximize your chance of hiring the best people while staying within your budget.

Steps in the hiring process

The following are typical steps in a hiring process:

1. Filling the funnel (i.e. recruiting and advertising)
2. Filtering and assessment
3. Interviewing
4. Decision making
5. Negotiation
6. Onboarding

Put another way, you want to get people interested enough to apply, figure out whom you want, then convince them to actually come work for you. In the list above, steps 2-4 have a lot of overlap. In this section we'll talk about how to structure this process, while going into much more depth about filtering, assessing, and interviewing in Chapters 6 and 7. We'll touch on onboarding in Chapter 8.

How you order and design each of these steps will depend largely on your expected incoming applicant volume. If you expect a low incoming volume of candidates you may want to start with resume scoring and then move to phone screening. If you have a very large volume of applicants, your primary concern is rapidly narrowing the candidate funnel. You may want to start with an automated, online assessment as the first step, as you may simply not have enough time to sort through all resumes in any meaningful way. Another method would be to automatically filter or score resumes with software, though this is a strategy that many find to be inadequate[24].

For assessments and interviews, you need to decide which specific skills and abilities of the candidates you want to test, how much

---

[24]As a data scientist, it's naturally tempting to want to go down the route of automatically scoring resumes using machine learning or similar techniques. The main issues facing this idea are the lack of good data, the large variation in how skills and experience are presented, and the ultimately free-form structure of resumes. This is not fundamentally impossible, seeing as humans can do a decent job, but is probably still in the realm of low accuracy and snake oil at the moment.

time and resources you can spend per candidate (and overhead), and who you will involve in the assessments and interviewing. In Chapters 6 and 7, we will go into more detail about which skills to assess and how to structure the assessments and interviews, but before that, you need to have a sense of how you want to set those up from a resources point of view:

- How will skills assessments be done?
  - Online, on the phone, on a (virtual?) whiteboard?
- Who will conduct the interviews?
- Will it be the same people on the interview loop for every candidate?
- Will you have a rotating team?
- How much time can or should these team members expect to dedicate to interviewing?
- What is your expected process time from application to offer?

Example structures

Here a are a couple of example structures. The first is one for a scenario in which you are expecting a very high volume of applicants. The second is aimed at a relatively low volume of applicants (either due to market conditions or due to screening that happens upstream from your process).

High volume, early-career level role

- Recruiting: a mix of contacting a small number of promising looking candidates directly, listing the job on major job boards, sponsoring a local event relevant to the role (e.g. a meetup on ML).
- Send most or all applicants an online basic skills assessment (auto-scored)

- Candidates scoring above the threshold on the automated assessment are invited to a short call with an HR representative and a hiring team representative.
  - HR covers some basic info (e.g. making sure the role, location, and work authorization are understood).
  - Hiring team member asks a few basic background and technical screening questions and answers questions about the team and role.
- Candidates advance to an on-site (or virtual on-site) interview.
  - More in-depth assessment of specific skills (e.g. programming, modeling, presenting, etc).
  - Introduction to hiring team members.
  - Introduction to non-hiring team members (i.e. people from other parts of the organization).
  - Team lunch.
  - More info from HR about benefits, etc.
  - Hiring manager meets with interview team to collect feedback and impressions.
- When a critical mass of well received candidates has made it through the entire process, rank candidates and start making offers.
- Negotiate and hopefully get an offer accepted.

For a high volume of applicants, a process structure like the above one has the benefit of automating the part of the funnel with the largest volume. The mechanics and details of this will be discussed in Chapters 6 and 7.

Low volume, senior hire

- Manual resume screening
- Invite promising candidates to a short call with an HR representative and a hiring team representative.

- HR covers some basic info (e.g. making sure the role, location, and work authorization are understood).
- Hiring team member asks a few basic background and technical screening questions and answers questions about the team and role.
  - Candidates advance to an on-site (or virtual on-site) interview.
    - Interviews cover technical aspects of role (e.g. programming, data work, modeling, and system design)
  - Introduction to hiring team members.
    - Introduction to non-hiring team members (i.e. people from other parts of the organization).
    - Team lunch.
    - More info from HR about benefits, etc.
    - Hiring manager meets with interview team to collect feedback and impressions.
  - When a critical mass of well received candidates has made it through the entire process, rank candidates and start making offers.
  - Negotiate and hopefully get an offer accepted.

For a low volume of candidates, in depth resume assessment is warranted and can be used as the step before moving directly to phone screens. The on-site interviews are largely similar, as you should have narrowed the funnel to a similar size at that point in the process, regardless of first stage funnel size, as the on-site is the least scalable part of your hiring process.

Making decisions

In Chapters 6 and 7 we will discuss how to formulate technical assessments and how to interview candidates. Sequential with those is the process of deciding which candidates to move forward in your process and eventually which ones to extend job offers to. In this section I'll cover considerations and strategies for making those decisions.

Narrowing the funnel

At the first stage of your hiring process (i.e. the top of the funnel), you will potentially have a large number of applicants. Your goal is to determine which are candidates most likely to help your organization succeed in its business goals and thrive. While it's possible you have a huge numbers of candidates that exceed your needs or no candidates that meet your needs, for the sake of structuring your hiring process, the primary "sizing" factor is your capacity to effectively move candidates through your hiring process in the time frame you need. In other words, regardless of how many applicants you start with, if your on-site capacity is four candidates per week, you need to aim to get down to that volume by that point in your funnel. This holds for all points in your funnel.

Avoid process bottlenecks

In one of my previous companies, one of the co-founders suggested that they personally call candidates that we identified as particularly promising. The idea was that the founder would be able to sell the candidate on the vision of the company and demonstrate our especially high level of interest in the candidate.

Candidates seemed to respond well to these calls. The only problem was that the co-founder was so busy with other high-priority work that the calls became a major bottleneck in our process. Realizing this, I talked to the co-founder and we agreed that, while useful, it had turned out to be an unrealistic idea and we removed that step from our process.

As previously mentioned, your process should never be looked at as a finished product, you need to constantly reconsider whether it's working as intended. In this case, we specifically had to identify where the bottlenecks were, as our hiring process was taking significantly longer than we wanted.

Setting thresholds

For assessments that you score on a point scale, you will likely want to set a threshold for candidates to move to the next stage if you are using the assessment as a filtering mechanism. This is especially true if you use an automatically scored online assessment as your first step for the scenario of a very large applicant volume.

There are two questions that come up in setting the threshold:

1. What do you want to achieve with the threshold?
2. What should the specific number be?

For the first question, you clearly want to filter for strong candidates[25], but more specifically what approximate fraction of the candidates should that be based on your screening capacity in the latter steps in the process and your overall hiring time frame? Are you trying to reduce you candidate pool by half at this point? By 90%?

For determining the specific number for your score threshold, it's unlikely that you will be able to confidently pick a number unless you already have a fair amount of data from previous assessment takers. In practice, this means that for a new assessment, you will

---

[25]We'll discuss more about what a "strong" candidate might mean in Chapters 6 and 7 and how well you can filter for them.

need to do some data sciencing: collect data for a while and then estimate the score threshold that will give you a funnel reduction of the magnitude you are aiming for. If this is taking too long, you may want to provisionally move some of the high scorers along, noting that the threshold has not yet been determined. You should also do some spot checking as you go. Are candidates that seem clearly below the skill level you are seeking making it past this stage? Are too few otherwise strong candidates making it through after you've decided on a threshold?

Decision making strategies

Like many things in hiring, how you decide to move a candidate forward, or especially how you decide to make a candidate an offer is something that solicits a very wide range of opinions. Also, like many things in hiring, it depends a lot on the size, culture, and structure or your organization.

Some teams will make the decision through a very democratic process, some will rely solely on the hiring manager, and some will come down to a cross-company hiring committee, with the ultimate decision made by someone not even within the department that is hiring. There are pros and cons to different approaches across this spectrum. I will list some of the decision strategies here with some pros, cons, and commentary.

Democratic process

By "democratic process", I mean that the team hiring votes on the candidates. The most extreme version of this is allowing any single team member to either veto or greenlight a candidate if they felt strongly enough.

Pros:

- Strong team buy-in.

- Potential to maintain and strengthen team culture.

Cons:

- Potential for perpetuating / entrenching bad aspects of the team culture.
- Potential for certain team members to have an outsized say in the case of veto or greenlight powers.
- Possibly slower decision making.

Hiring manager only

In this scenario the hiring manager is responsible for making the decision and holds all of the power.

Pros:

- Potentially very fast decision making.
- Manager can more holistically shape the team.

Cons:

- Potential for perpetuating / entrenching bad aspects of the team culture (especially cronyism).
- Potential for poor team buy-in.

Cross-company committee

This is most often found in large organizations that are striving to have a uniform process and standard for hires.

Pros:

- Potential for standardized quality bar across the organization

- Potential to strengthen company culture, rather than team-level culture.
- Potential to reduce cronyism.

Cons:

- Potential for slow decision making.
- Potential to hurt team-level culture.
- Potential for poor team buy-in.
- Very bureaucratic in feel.

Often a process like cross-company hiring committees are unavoidable once an organization grows to a certain size.

For smaller organizations, which have not yet grown into cross-company hiring committee territory, I recommend a process where the hiring team gives feedback to the hiring manager, who then synthesizes the information and makes a decision. Ideally, in part to promote buy-in, the hiring manager should present why they made the decisions and explicitly accept responsibility in the event that it turns out to be a mis-hire.

Summary

Hiring is about finding the best people for your organization's specific goals. The process you design to hire the best people needs to be created in the context of your specific hiring goals, available resources, constraints (e.g. time, money, regulatory, or bureaucratic constraints), and the state of the market for the roles you're hiring. By building a good understanding of your circumstances, you can then build a process aimed at maximizing your hiring chances and efficiency.

Interview: Sean Taylor, Lyft

Sean Taylor is a Data Science Manager at Lyft, where he leads Rideshare Labs. Before that he was at Facebook. Prior to working in data science, Sean completed a PhD in statistical social science from New York University.

You can find Sean online at seanjtaylor.com[a] and @seanjtaylor[b] on Twitter.

In the interview below, Sean discusses some of the main challenges faced by data science hiring managers and some of the approaches that he has used to address those challenges.

[a] https://seanjtaylor.com/
[b] https://twitter.com/seanjtaylor

Roy: Thanks for talking to me today about hiring in the realm of data science. Let's start off by having you give us some background on who you are and where you've gotten your experience.

Sean: Sure. Thanks. Currently I manage a data science team at Lyft, which is called Rideshare Labs. We have about twelve scientists on the team and work on a lot of open-ended projects that try to improve Lyft's marketplace efficiency and planning process. Before that I worked at Facebook for about seven years. I managed a statistics team there doing similar work, but in a very different domain. So I've been actively involved in hiring data scientists for a long time.

Roy: What was your pre-data science life?

Sean: Before Facebook I was a graduate student and I worked on social science research. Before that I was a software engineer for a couple years. I used to write a CRM type system in Python. A long time ago. And I also used to be a research assistant at the Federal Reserve Board, kind of an "economist to be".

Roy: You've been at Facebook and now at Lyft. That sounds like only a little, but in terms of data science that's a pretty long career. Over that time, what roles have you mostly hired for?

Sean: I have hired mostly for PhD research scientist type roles. The name of the role varies from company to company. Typically those are people with some specific research background. Maybe they're really good at forecasting or have a lot of experience with experimentation or things like that. I'm typically looking for data scientists that have strong coding skills. I personally prefer people that can come in and write code that we can put into production. That's been a big emphasis.

These are general purpose roles. I don't typically hire for a specific project, because I want someone to be around for a long time and be part of a team that evolves. In addition to a specific skill, I want just good generalists who are flexible and kind of interested in a wide space of problems.

Roy: Given that "data science" is such a broad term, when you say "generalists", are your generalists mostly focusing on statistical stuff? Or does your team also do machine learning?

Sean: Those things are all quite adjacent. I don't draw a hard line between them. People who have studied statistics are typically pretty good at machine learning. People who are good at machine learning, know a little bit of statistics. I don't think of those as mutually exclusive.

I think some domain knowledge in a deep topic that they've studied is important. I've got some operations research people on my team, which is new to me, but they are quite good data scientists. They just bring a different skill set to the table. There is a baseline knowledge of coding, data thinking, communication, visualization, etc, but also the deep expertise in a particular topic.

Roy: When I think about Sean Taylor, I think of forecasting and experimentation. You're one of the people I know who works at a big company, where very focused specialization is possible, but it seems like you need whatever the most applicable techniques are and the field is evolving very quickly, so it makes sense to be very broad.

Sean: Those two things that you know about me are like two chapters of a something like an eight chapter book. I think of data science as periods of deep focus on some problem, but then you move problem to problem quite regularly.

Roy: A lot of re-invention going on.

Sean: Yeah, you kind of collect little case studies of stuff that you worked on. There are some similarities between problems. I hope those are leverageable, but sometimes they're not.

Roy: What do you see as the biggest challenges in hiring for these roles?

Sean: I think one of the hardest things is extrapolation of the experiences that people have had. When I'm hiring someone out of graduate school, I'm taking one or two projects that they've worked on in a deep way and asking "because they were capable of doing this in that environment, will they be capable of doing it in this new environment?" That's pretty challenging. Because data science is quite different from role to role and company to company, there's this portability problem. How can I know that the skill set is going to translate.

That's why I think finding people who have worked on many diverse projects is a really strong signal. It says that they've had to go through the rinse-repeat process. Learning how to ask good questions in a new domain. Learning the tools that they need. Delivering results. If you can do that more than once, that's a pretty strong signal that you can do it in a new environment.

Roy: What have you seen in your career that's changed related to data science hiring?

Sean: At the beginning, eight or ten years ago, it felt like the whole interview process was just completely borrowed from software engineering. It was like coding, plus a little bit of analytics questions, and that would get you a job as a data scientist. Now I think we've gotten better at customizing the interview to capture more of the data science specific skills. It used to be more buzzword centric. "Do you know Hadoop? And if you don't then we can't hire you, because you're gonna need Hadoop right away." I think we've gotten more tool agnostic. I barely even look at the technical skills section on people's resumes. I just assume you're going to have to learn some new tool almost every month of your job. Getting more tool agnostic has been sort of a trend.

People certainly just have more experience now. If you looked at resumes six or seven years ago, you had this portability thing I was talking about. They were coming from a totally different field, like financial modeling, and it was hard to know if they were going to be a good data scientist. Now there are people with a really strong data science track record. So you can see more highly relevant projects.

These are all good signs. It's easier to find good people and easier for people to signal that they can do their work.

Roy: How does a candidate come across your desk?

Sean: At a big company like Facebook or Lyft there is a whole recruiting team and there are people called sourcers. A sourcer's job is to find resumes for you to look at. You work closely with the sourcer to explain what you're looking for. They are not usually super technical people, so you explain roughly what you're looking for in a candidate and hope they can kind of internalize that.

To be honest I get a lot of inbound emails, often from friends of friends, looking for jobs. There's in internal quality signal there, but you need to worry some about bias.

From resume to interview, I've got to figure out if this is someone that's likely to pass our interview process. That's a level dependent thing. Internally at these companies there are levels denoting different amounts of seniority. The interview process is tailored to the level, so if I'm hiring for a "level 6" role, that person is going to have to pass a very stringent set of interviews, so I'm looking for a ton of experience, somebody who can clearly demonstrate that they can get a job like that. All the filters involved is a lot. The story I've heard is that there's something like a 10x drop off at each phase.

Roy: Does that count cold applicants?

Sean: Yeah. The cold applicants are going through the sourcer. Periodically I'll help source. We'll go through LinkedIn or Twitter and try to find people that look like they'd be good fits for the role. Lots of people apply through the website. There are great candidates that come in through cold applications. They're at a little disadvantage, compared to ones that we're actively sourcing, because they're lumped in a pile with a lot of lower quality candidates. We do look at every resume to some extent, though.

Roy: Where do you spend the most time in the hiring process?

Sean: The thing that is always the most expensive is interviewing time. For a candidate we'll do something like five 45 minute or hour long interviews. I'll be on at least one of the interviews for a candidate for my team. We interview probably five to ten times as many candidates as we hire. Accounting for per hire time, I probably spend at least five hours at the interviewing stage. The actual screening steps are a little lighter weight. The things that you can do in a smaller amount of time. But when you commit to interviewing somebody, you really want to give them a fair shot at getting the role.

It's not just interviewing, you need to then go write your feed-back and then meet as a set of interviewers and discuss how to triangulate the feedback. At Lyft we have something called Hiring

Committee, so candidates that meet the bar through the hiring committee are subjected to another committee to make sure we keep a standard across the whole organization. I've been on the Hiring Committee for about a year. I spend most of my time in these meetings trying to compress the information from interviews into decisions. That's an extremely time consuming process.

Roy: What would be your main pieces of advice to other hiring managers to do the best job of hiring?

Sean: Do a lot of exploratory interviews. That's my favorite tool. It's really hard to get a lot of information from a resume. I think of it almost like a classifier. You have type I or type II errors: false positives or false negatives. There's no substitute for just talking to someone and hearing about what they've been working on. There's lots of great advice on how to get value from those exploratory interviews. I love a thirty minute phone call with a candidate. Often you can see if it's a good fit just by asking them what they're looking for.

The part of the resume that nobody really writes anymore is the objective, which I was coached to write when I was younger. "What kind of role are you looking for?" I don't think people do that as much anymore. But you can actually avoid them making a mistake by starting on a process that's not likely to lead to a role that they want.

In economics terms there is vertical differentiation and horizontal differentiation. Some candidates are just stronger than others and you should always prefer stronger candidates to weaker candidates. But then there is this fit dimension: are they going to get to work on the stuff that they want to for their career?

Roy: Maybe they're great at SQL, but they don't actually want an "all SQL, all the time" role.

Sean: Exactly. People being interested in the work that they're actually doing is probably one of the strongest predictors of career success. I really think that just having the conversation about what they really want is important. The resume is retrospective, right? But what you're looking for is a prospective signal.

Back when we could go in the office I would invite prospective candidates to come to Lyft for lunch. That was a useful tool for figuring out if we should start this expensive process of a day long interview and all of the stuff that comes with that.

Roy: Speaking of the office, is your team now hiring remote? How has that altered your process?

Sean: Most of our interviews are now video call based. It's a challenge. We're still learning how to do that well. The hardest part is lack of a whiteboard or collaborative surface to problem solve with. We have tried different things there and none of them have been great. Particularly anything that involves diagramming or light-weight math. I think whiteboard coding is actually quite bad. Moving to something like CoderPad, where you are typing into something that more closely approximates where you would normally write code, is an improvement. But some things are not an improvement.

I think for candidate experience, it's quite challenging. It kind of dehumanizes someone when they're over a video call. You still need to offer to let them take a bio-break, for example. Just because they're on a call doesn't mean they don't need to go get some water or use the bathroom. We're getting better at it, but it's been an ongoing process.

Roy: Any other pieces of advice that you would give to hiring managers?

Sean: One of the things I think a lot about is candidate experience. The humanization of people who are going through the process is one of the most important things you can do. You look at a bajillion resumes. You interview a bajillion people. They're all people hoping that this will be the next phase of their career - a place where they'll be for a few years. I think making people feel comfortable, like they feel understood, that they feel the process was fair to them, is one of the most important things you can do. It affects the reputation of your company and your reputation. And if the person gets hired, you're going to work with them! All of these are great reasons to try to make the process as friendly as possible. I don't think there's any real substitute for thinking deeply about that.

The other thing that I think a lot about is that interview processes should closely approximate what they'll be doing on the job. When we ask people coding questions, people tend to lose the thread and focus on "they need to be good at coding questions". No, they need to be good at the tasks that they're going to be doing on the job. A coding question is a proxy for that.

Designing good interview questions is a lot about thinking about what is the work that I expect this person to succeed at. We're very lucky at Lyft to have a large team of people working on redesigning our interview process pretty regularly. Thinking about whether these questions really capture on the job things that we expect people to do. You pay a lot of up front effort to make those questions capture what you want and write rubrics. If you do that well it's a better value for everybody. People end up in jobs that they're more likely to succeed at and you're more likely to have candidates that will be successful at your company.

Roy: I think that it's really difficult. There's a tension between doing something that's as close as possible to the day-to-day work and a more abstract approach, trying to distill the fundamental skills into some other kind of test.

Sean: It's a kind of factor analysis, but you can over-regularize and end up with too few factors.

[Nerd laughter]

Roy: Thanks a lot for sitting down for this interview, Sean.

Sean: You're welcome!

Chapter 5: Job descriptions and resumes

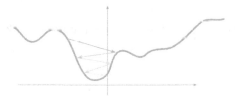

When hiring for a specific role, the job description is one of the most important things that you will need to produce. It is used to attract and inform potential applicants, used by your organization in advertizing and recruiting, and can play a huge roll in the success of your hiring. The key is creating a job description that is as specific and informative as possible for the position you are trying to fill.

Candidates, on the other hand, typically submit a resume as part of their application. The resume is similar to the job description, in that it is trying to convey as much useful (and positive sounding) information as possible in a small amount of space.

In this chapter I will discuss how to create effective job descriptions and how to use resumes in your hiring process. I will focus on aspects that are of specific importance for data science and machine learning engineering hiring, but also cover a number of more generic aspects.

Writing an effective job description

The most important role of a job description (i.e. job advertisement) is to catch the interest of potential applicants and inform them of the specifics of the role. Additionally, you want to inform them about the team and broader organization, as well as things like benefits and perks. You want to simultaneously give the potential applicants a good understanding of the role, while getting them excited about the prospect of working on your team. Ideally, you will increase your candidate "signal-to-noise ratio" by helping potential applicants understand the role well and allowing them to self-select, instead of just getting an application from every person out there who is slightly interested in DS or MLE roles.

Choosing a job title

The most important aspect of the job description is probably the title of the job itself. As discussed previously, you should very intentionally work to understand your business problems, the likely tasks involved in solving those problems, and then choose the most appropriate role to help you achieve those goals.

In choosing a title, you want to be as clear and descriptive as possible. This may mean a relatively narrow title and adding a modifier to make it more specific, e.g. "Machine Learning Engineer - ML infrastructure". Even with a broader role, you should try to be as explicit as possible. For example, if you need to hire someone to perform a very wide set of data science related tasks, instead of the vague title of "Data Scientist" you might instead choose the title "Generalist Data Scientist" or "Full-stack Data Scientist".

In some organizations you may have little room to customize the name of a role. At some companies, for example, an MLE or even a DS may have an official title like "Software Engineer III". Depending on your organization's policy, you may still be able to advertize that role under a more descriptive title. In other cases, you may opt for a more descriptive title and the final, official title of the person you hire may end up as part of the hiring negotiation.

> ### Good job titles are no guarantee
>
> At one company we posted a job ad with the title "Machine Learning Specialist". Amusingly we ended up with several applicants who, rather then being skilled at machine learning, were actually machinists.
>
> No matter how good your title or job description is, you will still get some number of people who just apply without bothering to pay attention to the details.

My suggestion is, if at all possible, chose a very descriptive title. Don't go with cutesy titles like "Data Ninja" or "AI Rockstar". These are likely to turn off some serious candidates.

Creating a good job description

As mentioned in the beginning of this section, the most important goals of a job description is to catch the interest of potential candidates and inform them about the role, team, and company. For data science and machine learning roles, clearly describing the role and the expected skills is especially important. Let's look at some of the specific material that you will likely want to include.

> ### What do candidates really care about in a job ad? The company name.
>
> If you ask candidates what they are most looking for in a job ad, in my experience the most common answer is "brand name".

They recognize the company or organization as a desireable place to work, before knowing anything about the job specifics. It's hard to escape the power of the brand name. Clearly some "brands" will appeal more to some than others (even to extent of being the reason for some to actively ignore the ad).

What can you do here? Not a ton in the short term. Building your brand is moving a large stone that's mostly beyond the reach of the typical DS or MLE manager. A couple of strategies that have helped some relatively unknown companies to build their brands as good places to work for data scientists and MLE's are blogging[a] on technical topics related to the team's work and hosting events. The key is consistently marketing these aspects. As with everything, the ROI of these efforts should be re-evaluated regularly.

---

[a]Stitch Fix is an example of a company that successfully built a brand as an employer of data scientists via their extensive blogging, even to the point of becoming the target of parody, which of course indicates that they have achieved a large mind share.

You will want to describe several aspects of the role you are seeking to fill. Below are some of the most common types of information that you are likely to want to provide.

High-level information:

- The high-level mandate of the role (e.g. building models to forecast service demand)
- General technical tasks (e.g. developing, deploying, and maintaining time series based forecasting models for internal consumption, working with data engineering team to specify data flow needs, etc.)
- Basic role information (e.g. full-time, location, remote, level, etc.)

Technical specifics:

- Specific technical tasks (e.g. A/B testing of mobile app features)
- Languages and technologies (just the highlights)
- Most important techniques (e.g. NLP with neural networks)
- Basic skills and knowledge expected
- Nice to have skills and knowledge

Team, company, and culture:

- The overall mission and status of the company or organization.
- Which team and department the role is on.
- General company culture aspects and practices that affect day-to-day work, for example:
    - "We take off every other Friday."
    - "We have a very flat org structure."
    - "We are fully distributed and work asynchronously."
    - "We put a premium on in-office, face to face teamwork."

Benefits and perks (examples[26]):

- Unlimited vacation with mandatory minimum.
- Flexible work hours.
- Generous retirement account contribution.
- Fully paid health insurance.
- 6 month parental leave.
- Build your own [home] workstation, including the hardware and OS or your choice.
- Annual, optional company off-sites.

Logistics:

---

[26]Some of these examples are very specific to US employers. Highlight the benefits and perks that you offer as an employer for the region you're hiring in.

- If remote, clarification on what that means (examples):
  - Fully remote, with quarterly team get togethers.
  - Remote with one day per week in the office.
  - Remote, but must be within +/- 2 hours of our time zone.
  - Remote, but employees must be within the EU.
- Whether visa support is available.
- Travel expectations.
- Full-time, permanent versus contract, etc.
- Degree requirements (usually a bad idea)

The above are a good starting place for creating a strong description. There are a few other things to keep in mind.

Often HR will want to include boilerplate, insist on approval, or even insist that they write the description themselves. At the least, you should express to them what you think are the most important aspects for your roles, especially if you think they are materially different than what HR would typically put down for other roles. Optimally, the team doing the hiring should be the primary author of the job description and have final sign-off.

Using AI to improve job ads

There are several online services that purport to be able to improve your job ad by applying their specialized AI to revise the ad copy. I recommend that your save your money. Fundamentally it's unlikely that these companies have access to the datasets that they would need to actually build reasonable "AI" (i.e. a very large dataset of job ads along with information about the resulting applicant pools and the outcomes of the eventual hires.)

I instead recommend that you invite a handful of knowledgeable co-workers or outsiders to review your ad copy and make any suggestions.

If you are a non-data science person who is tasked with hiring or creating the job description, make sure you are confident about the technologies and skills that you are listing. Try to get feedback from someone more knowledgeable. Otherwise you run the risk of turning off potential candidates that see errors in the technical side as a red flag. The classic example is asking for people to have more years of experience using some technology than that technology has actually existed.

How specific should you be?

One of the concerns hiring managers rightly have is scaring away potentially promising candidates by being so specific about the job requirements that it looks like an impossible match for anyone. The temptation can be to go too far into the direction of "we just want some hard-working, smart people", who may need an unmanageable amount of time to get up to speed (not to say that this isn't the right solution in some scenarios).

I recommend that you try to tier the needed skills and experience, such as having "fundamental required skills", "skills we will teach you", and "nice to haves". Clearly candidates with all of those on day one will be better matches, but it also helps you attract a broader range of candidates, while being able to differentiate them better and communicating your culture of learning and growth.

Reviewing resumes

Resumes[27] and cover letters are the candidate's equivalent of the job description. They want to convey as much relevant and interesting information about themselves as possible in a small amount of space. While the resume can function as a "ad" for the candidate, one major difference can simply be the scale of volume of resumes versus job ads. A job seeker may look at tens or possibly hundreds of job ads, but an organization looking to hire a data science related role in 2021 may be faced with hundreds or thousands (or more!) of resumes and cover letters. This means that having a strategy of how to handle these is important.

Once again, we are faced with an optimization problem weighing your constraints, resources, and goals. If you are in a position to have a team of screeners from HR, you personally may need to view very few resumes. If you are in a small company, you may be faced with thousands of applications and no one to help you process the resumes. You need to figure out the best way to extract signal from the volume of resumes you are facing *and* do that in a fair way.

Assessing resumes is inherently difficult. There are three main strategies for dealing with resumes:

1. Human assessment
2. Automated assessment (in various degrees)
3. Non-assessment

Below we'll discuss some of the pros and cons of each strategy.

Human assessment of resumes

If you have a low ratio of resumes to people who can assess them (i.e. either few applicants or lots of people to review them), the most

---

[27]Depending on your location, this may be the equivalent of a curriculum vitae, or CV.

common strategy is to have people review each resume.

Pros:

- Humans are good at understanding the contents and at dealing with unusual formatting, etc.
- Humans can quickly get a sense of how an individual resume compares to the larger set of resumes.

Cons:

- Humans are slow and expensive for this kind of task.
- Humans need to be trained for what to look for.
- Humans are biased and inconsistent when performing this kind of task.

If having people look at applicant resumes is practical for your situation, how can you make it work best? The answer is probably standardization. You need to create a standard process and scoring rubric for the people assessing the resumes to use. A rubric might give sub scores to things like:

- Evidence of knowledge of topics X, Y, and Z.
- Evidence of experience performing tasks A, B, and C.
- Evidence of experience learning new skills on the job.

The rubric can be used to give relatively standard scores in each of the categories and then weigh those category scores for a combined total score. As with all formulaic methods, you will need to decide on score thresholds and figure out how to deal with certain edge cases.

Reducing bias in assessing resumes

On a basic level you want to have a fair process for assessing resumes and there is a lot of potential for bias. Ultimately you want to hire the best people for your team and your organization, but it's easy to get in your own way.

Some common strategies are doing things like removing candidates' names from resumes or even the names of where (or when) they got there education or work experience. This can help to reduce some bias, though it can require the applicant to separately re-enter the information from their resume.

In some countries it is common to add a lot of personal information to a resume, such as a picture, marital status, date of birth, place of birth, etc. These are also things to consider removing from resumes to reduce the chance of bias, as they are largely immaterial to the role under question (and in jurisdictions such as the US they expose you to legal risk).

Another technique to reduce bias is by having multiple reviewers. While this can have the benefit of combatting the bias (and inconsistency) of any single reviewer, it also obviously drives up the "cost" of reviewing resumes.

When creating a resume scoring rubric, you should attempt to create categories the capture what skills and experience you feel is required for the candidate to move to the next phase of the hiring process. There should be enough room in the scoring to allow you to both differentiate candidates, and to adjust your threshold if you are advancing too many or too few candidates.

Some example scoring categories might be:

- Evidence of ML knowledge (0 - 3 points)
- Evidence of programming experience (0 - 3 points)

- Evidence of real-world ML experience (0 - 3 points)
- Evidence of outstanding professional or academic achievement (0 - 3 points)
- Evidence of the ability and drive to learn on their own (0 - 3 points)
- Overall impression (0 - 3 points)

These are of course highly dependent on the role you're hiring for and does not eliminate all of the potential issues when manually screening resumes. As with all of these methods, you should periodically do a spot check on a random sample of the resumes you're assessing to determine if the rubric-based scores "feel" right. Are there resumes that everyone agrees are strong, but are getting low scores (and vice-versa)?

Automated assessment of resumes

Automation of resume assessment can range from searching the pool of applicant resumes, to filtering based on keywords, to using "AI" to score resumes for you.

Pros:

- Scalable and fast.
- Can be easy to use and automated.

Cons:

- Can be very inaccurate.
- Can be expensive.
- Can create new biases or re-enforce current biases (e.g. filtering by university).

Using automation to help screen resumes is a very alluring prospect, but it has a lot of potential pitfalls. The classic mistake is creating filters that are much too rigid (e.g. rejecting a great candidate who is missing one required keyword) or narrow. With more advanced, ML-based techniques, you can easily run into the problems that are inherent in ML systems: poor quality training data, training data that is dissimilar to your data, a model optimized to solve a different problem than the one your faced with, etc.

If you go the route of automation, you need to be confident that the criteria you are choosing are really what you need to filter on for the role you are hiring for. As with all of these methods, you should periodically assess a sample of resumes by hand to see if the filtering or scoring makes intuitive sense.

Non-assessment of resumes

Finally we get to what might seem like the most radical option with regards to resumes: not using them to filter candidates.

Why would you not use resumes as a basis for filtering candidates? The answer is two-fold: volume and fairness. If you have too many applications to perform resume-screening in a practical amount of time, you might consider simply not assessing resumes. This also has the advantage of eliminating bias that exists in resume screening.

Pros:

- The fastest method of dealing with resumes.
- Eliminates the bias that can exist in resume assessment.

Cons:

- You need to create something else that serves as a funnel narrowing mechanism at this stage in the hiring process.

- It may be difficult to convince HR or others to use this strategy.
- Candidates may feel like all of their effort going into resume crafting is in vain.

As alluded to in the "Cons" above, this strategy does not mean that you just advance every applicant past the first stage. Instead you need a mechanism to narrow the funnel. The most common way to do that is to have candidates take a technical skills assessment as the first step of the process. Some organizations have even made that part of the application process itself. I will spend a substantial portion of the next chapter discussing strategies for skills assessment.

Moving from non-assessment to manual assessment and back again

In one role as a hiring manager I had decided to send a take-home assessment to all applicants that looked minimally potentially qualified. What I was not prepared for was the shear applicant volume. Suddenly I needed a new strategy, because the time needed to score all of the take-homes would have been impossible. At that point I decided to screen resumes.

To be as consistent and fair as possible, I designed a resume scoring rubric and set out assessing resumes. The goal was to spend a couple minutes per resume, rather than the 30+ minutes it could take to assess a take-home submission.

This served as a stop gap measure, but ultimately was not sustainable or scalable as I was the only person available to score resumes and the volume continued to grow. The solution was to redesign the process, skipping the resume assessment step, but automating as much of the rest as possible.

Ultimately the candidate's resume will play a role, even in a "non-assessment" strategy. In that case the resume will act more are an additional piece of information when interviewing the candidate later stages of the process, rather than as something to directly filter against.

Of all the strategies mentioned above, applicant volume and available human resources are the main determining factors. For lower applicant volume roles, the more scalable processes may not be necessary, but you should consider your options to decide what is the best for your situation, fairly filtering for the best candidates.

Summary

In this chapter we've looked at how to craft an effective job description and how to effectively assess (or not assess!) resumes. These are crucial pieces in your overall hiring strategy and process.

In the next two chapters we will look at some of the most difficult, controversial, and important steps in hiring data scientists and machine learning: skills assessment and interviewing.

Interview: Angela Bassa, iRobot

Angela Bass is the Senior Director of the Data Science and Analytics Center of Excellence at iRobot. Prior to iRobot she worked in several roles as a consultant across a diverse set of industries, applying her mathematical skills to help organizations make important strategic decisions. She has a bachelor's degree in math from MIT.

You can find Angela online at angelabassa.com[a] and @AngeBassa[b] on Twitter.

In the interview below, Angela discusses her wide range of experiences as both an individual contributor and as a manager. She touches on some of the main challenges faced by data science hiring managers and some of the approaches that she has used to address those challenges.

[a] https://www.angelabassa.com/
[b] https://twitter.com/AngeBassa

Roy: Let's start by having you give us some info about your background.

Angela: Sure. I am the Senior Director of the Data Science and Analytics Center of Excellence at iRobot, which is a mouthful. In essence it means that all of the analytics and data science goodness that happens at iRobot happens with a bunch of people that are smarter than me, that I have conned into joining me on this great adventure.

Roy: I'm not gonna believe that. The conning part or the smarter than you part.

Angela: The part about them being smarter than me is legit. 100%. From top to bottom. From the CEO, whose signature is etched in metal on Mars as we speak, to the interns, who are driving lots of the actual innovation with the crazy ideas that they bring.

How did I get here? In a circuitous way. There isn't really a direct path to data science management. The first data science majors only started in the last decade. When you ask someone about being an accountant, you know exactly what the career path will be. Data science is a little bit weirder and rounder and curvier.

I started out in math. I have a math degree and Wall Street recruits pretty heavily out of math programs. So I worked there for a while. That was a terrible idea – just a really bad personality fit. Nothing against the folks who work there, but for me it was just not a good fit. But I did learn a lot about business and how data is used in business decision making and in defining and driving strategy. For somebody who was just coming out of their egg shell, it was really useful knowledge, because it gave me a context later on about how this kind of work would actually be seen by people three, four, five layers above me, who don't have a lot of context. That was us on Wall Street with very little context, just looking at numbers.

After that I worked on strategy for a small consulting firm and did that for several years. That was really interesting, because I just parachuted into problems. You don't really see the boring, the water cooler. No company is going to bring in consultants when things are fine! That was very interesting as an external participant.

Roy: What kind of work were you doing as a consultant?

Angela: The first firm that I joined was doing pharmaceutical strategy. Working in different therapeutic areas, looking at disease indications. How do you stage clinical trials so that you discharge risk in order get a molecule through regulators? Some of those clinical trials can be *extremely* expensive. So who's gonna pay me, someone with a math degree, to help them with their decisions? People who have really big decisions that the need help with.

Roy: So were you doing things like risk modeling?

Angela: Yes. Risk modeling. Also, when you're structuring claims to present to regulatory bodies, like the FDA, on what a medication does or does not do, you have to set up your statistical trials in a very specific way to demonstrate certain thresholds, etc. I did some pre-registration, some financial modeling, some competitive intelligence. I ran the gambit.

Then I did some agricultural work: some genetic trait introgression and modeling growth yields of soybeans, etc. Then later I worked in energy. I worked in marketing services for an organization that sold their services to big brands – coupons and what not. And then I worked at EnerNOC, which was really fun. That's an energy company.

And then iRobot called and the six year old in me was like, "I'm sorry, what? Robots? Yes! Please and thank you!". And here we are.

Roy: When did you transition for being an individual contributor to management?

Angela: So my first role as a manager was at the strategy consulting firm, but I had a bad experience. It took a while before I decided to test those waters again. It was not until several years later at a different firm, at the marketing services organization, that I actually had folks reporting to me, where I was evaluating their performance, etc. Before then I had been an engagement manager. I had led projects and had teams of people on those projects, but junior consultants didn't report to me. I didn't own the P&L [28]. The first time that I did was later on. I was as manager at EnerNOC and then a manager at iRobot.

Roy: When was your first experience with hiring as a manager?

---

[28]Profit and loss.

Angela: That was at the marketing services organization. Going through the process of not just being part of an interview panel or an evaluation panel, but actually writing the job description, procuring the funds, making the case, onboarding, training, evaluating, growing, developing, assigning tasks, all of that good stuff.

Roy: What kinds of roles were you hiring for?

Angela: In that role my title was Director of the Analytic Group. That's when I started hiring "data analysts", "data quality", and I think "database administrators" were the titles. This was in the early 2010's.

Roy: As you moved along, everyone started shifting over to the term "data science"?

Angela: To be honest, I had not heard the term "data science" at the time. The term hadn't really been a term that I had heard yet. I had started working with groups like R Ladies and tutoring people in R at meetups and things. Then a meetup group called something like Data Science Boston popped up. I went and met a whole bunch of interesting professionals with different, weird titles, who were doing the kind of work that I wanted to be doing at the intersection of mathematics and large volumes of data. People were talking about pattern matching strategies that had been developed at companies that suddenly had had enough data to push the envelope.

Then I met with the folks from EnerNOC at one of those events and they recruited me to come in and set up the data science function for them. That went on for about two and a half years. It was a great experience. Unfortunately they ran out of runway and had to do layoffs. And data science was the tip of the spear. If you're not a data science company, if you're exploring, it's a substantial investment, but takes a little bit to mature. It was unfortunate. It was a really good crew.

Roy: So you went from the early days, which was more data analyst and DBA based, but then the titles started to change.

Angela: I don't know that it's just new titles. I think the roles have changed. The objectives, the skill sets have changed.

Roy: The tools have also changed. Everything.

Angela: Yes. I'm glad that the terminology is evolving to match. I still hire data analysts. I still hire people focused on data quality. We have different names depending on the different applications. But now at iRobot the scope is much broader. We have machine learning engineers and data engineers and data platform managers and performance analysts and testing analysts. So there's more specialization, because it's a much bigger organization.

Roy: What do you think is the biggest challenge in hiring data science and machine learning roles?

Angela: A big challenge in hiring for these kinds of roles is just the volume of applicants. This is a great problem to have. But you can't go on YouTube to learn how to be a surgeon. Or blogs or just textbooks. There's some apprenticeship required for most skills. In data science that "apprenticeship" can be digital and asynchronous. So it's just such a low barrier to entry into such a lucrative profession that has high demand.

But that means that we have to be much more mindful and deliberate about how we hire. It takes concerted, intentional effort to decide what are the skills that I still need, given what my business needs to accomplish, given the team I already have on my bench, given all of the different bits of context. What is it that I need to go out into the market and find? And then being honest about what's the "nice to have", what's the "need to have", and what are the intangibles. What am I missing? I need someone with this particular skill set. I need someone with Python and SQL and the specific skills. But maybe I also need someone with a specific methodological approach. Maybe someone who understands ethnography a little bit. Somebody who understands qualitative methods. Somebody who understands signal loss when you're going from qualitative to quantitative methods. Somebody who has done conjoint analyses in field.

Why is my team today the envy of the industry? We have marine biologists - people who know how to model a system.

Roy: The people who help your vacuum cleaner avoid the aquarium?

Angela: Among other things! They learned how to model systems, where the only thing they had where the artifacts of a dolphin existing. A dolphin can't tell you why certain actions were taken. That literature exists. I was oblivious to that. Here's someone who can come in and teach us. We wouldn't have found it on our own. We needed someone who could open the door to all of that knowledge.

We have statisticians. We have somebody with an ethnomusicology degree - somebody who deeply understands how to create systems culturally, which is important for us, because we have an entire globe using our products. We manufacture them for everyone, but there's seven billion of us. How do we understand our customers?

We have teams focused on privacy and security and stewardship and regulatory compliance. All those things. We have to value contributions that go beyond the tactical execution of the work and writing those into the job description. Saying explicitly that these are things that we want. Which are the skill sets that I need somebody with mastery? Which are skill sets that are required, but there is room for learning? Which are skill sets that just having familiarity with is enough? Just being really honest about that. I think that helps attract candidates who are more self-aware and who are a better fit. So that helps with the volume problem.

The second big problem is having a really strong network. Not just so you can hire people who look like you or who walk your walk or know your people, but establishing a broad enough network so that I have both friends and colleagues, but also strangers helping me find people that I can't find by myself. One of the reasons to do podcasts, to go out and speak, to have a public profile, to have a voice out there is so that people will trust that I am going to be a good steward of somebody's career and growth, even if we haven't met in person. There's a track record there. That helps me find those talents from schools that I didn't attend, from other disciplines, etc.

Roy: Given the huge population of potential candidates for these jobs, do you have preferred (or non-preferred) methods that you like to use for assessing candidate's skills?

Angela: This is a really difficult question. I'm not a fan of asking people to do work that they're not getting paid to do as part of an interview process. It feels strange to me that you're getting people to jump through hoops. But, the flip side is I've had an experience where that wasn't in place and we did verbal interviews and we asked all of the questions and there was no coding aspect to the interview. We had a person pass with flying colors, but then they started and they didn't know how to do the work! They just didn't know it. It was so difficult and unnecessary. We've put a test in place.

The way that we do our coding challenge is to use a comprehensive test. If someone were to answer everything it would take them a good ten hours. It's long. So we tell people "don't do the whole thing." Part of what we're assessing is "what do you choose to work on?". Do you choose to tackle the hard stuff first? Do you choose to tackle something that will give you context? Do you choose to tackle something that you have familiarity with? Do you choose to do things in order, because you assume there is some editorial reason for why the questions are ordered the way that they are? How do you structure your solutions? Are you setting yourself up for the whole project or are you tackling things piecemeal? Whatever it is, that will help us when we sit down to talk to you about your coding challenge. We can then talk about more than just "do you know how to use addition?" We can talk about "why did you tackle this problem this way?" "What were you trying to do?" That is just a much more informative conversation.

Roy: How do you score that assessment?

Angela: We have an assessment with the questions and the data set. That data set is very representative of what we do. It's a synthetic data set, but it has the structure of our real data. Part of the assessment is what questions you have about the data. We're giving you a very real look at what the day-to-day is going to be. "Is this something that excites you and motivates you?" So it's not just a rubric or a pass-fail. What did you not get right? Some foundational concept, or did you forget a semicolon or run out of time and you just wanted to submit it, because you're still excited about it? So there's not like a pass-fail, but we do know what the answers are supposed to be.

Roy: How do you select which candidates get to that stage in the first place, to take the assessment? I assume you don't send that to every applicant.

Angela: It's a lot a work to assess the challenge. Because somebody took the time to invest in that, the least we can do is take the time to invest in constructive feedback. So we don't send it to everyone who applies. It would just overwhelm us.

Who gets that is the toughest part. The assessment is easy. Interviewing is easy. We have certain questions that we ask: "do you move with urgency?", "do you pursue possibilities?", "do you have your team's back?", "are you customer centric?" There are all sorts of big picture things that we look at. There are very job specific things that we look at too. "Can you do the work that you're going to have to do?" "Do you know how to code in the language that we code in?" "Are you familiar with the concepts that we need you to be familiar with?" All of that is easy to ask once someone gets in the door.

Getting in is why we have a phenomenal talent acquisition team internally at iRobot. They spoil us greatly. They have college outreach programs and a robust STEM education program that helps feed talent into the organization. We have internship programs here in Boston. We work with local boot camps and organizations that train folks. We let them know when we have new openings.

Folks who just apply on LinkedIn or whatever got through an internal system that looks for the bare minimum set of requirements. Then we have our internal team do an initial screening and then the hiring manager does a phone screening. We have screening questions that we've all agreed to. If a candidate is moved forward from there, then they get the assessment. If they do well on the assessment, then we invite them to a round of interviews.

Roy: It's always interesting to hear how people structure things and how they deal with those different problems: volume and the ambiguous backgrounds of candidates.

Once you've actually hired people, how do you set them up for success?

Angela: I think it depends. For a very small team a lot of structure is probably not very helpful. There's probably a lot of ad hoc questions that come in and trying to impose structure to a team that needs to be dynamic and flexible is counterproductive. When you reach a level of scale where you need that predictability and consistency and planning, it's a different set of things that set someone up for success.

It's just being really intentional. When I started at iRobot, our onboarding process was essentially twelve weeks of EDA [29]. We had the "Summer of Lunch and Learns". We were all onboarding ourselves and each other. It was all brand new. Now I don't think that that would work for us. I think the pace would be off and we wouldn't be even able to bring as many people together for that long a stretch of time. We're indispensible now. We can't just go spelunking anymore. We were bootstrapped before, but now we're plugged into the machinery. So for people who now join to get a very specific task done we have really good processes to help them come up to speed.

---

[29]Exploratory data analysis

The other thing is creating culture, especially in this pandemic, covid world. How do you get people to remember that they work with *people*. It's not just pixels and emails and slack messages. Making sure that it's not just happy hours, but a sense of comradery and knowing who's working on what and who you can learn from. Not just the "fake" time to come together. You need all of the other stuff that turns that "fake" time into "real" time. You want it to be an organic thing that people want to do, rather than just a calendar invite, that half the people don't show up to, because they don't feel like they're part of a group bigger than themselves.

It's not a family. It's a business. It's a corporate relationship, *but* it's a corporate relationship of people who have the same mission, who want to come together, who have similar values, and who can do really good work. You want to frame it openly, honestly, and intentionally.

Roy: So what if people don't set up the self-organized stuff?

Angela: They won't at first. Especially in this industry there's a self-selection of introverts, who are over-represented. That's what I mean about being more intentional. There are folks who will come to the online coffee or lunches. But there are folks who won't. What will those folks come to? Do I need to set up a trivia game? Is it family time? Is it more about the work rather than play time? So making intentional opportunities for knowledge transfer. Having the all hands and reiterating over and over what the strategy is, so that folks feel like they are hearing the message and in our own language. Putting in the elbow grease to have that team feel connected.

Roy: A very multi-faceted approach. You need to try to do all of those things?

Angela: It is! And it feels a lot like emotional labor. It feels a lot like cheerleading.

There are two things that are really important with teams: psychological safety and engagement. You can be as safe as you want to be, but if you're not motivated, you're just going to be safely sitting in your chair and not going above and beyond. You have to feel safe and to trust that you can throw a dumb idea out and nobody's gonna chew you out for it. But you have to feel motivated to throw it! That motivation doesn't happen organically. When you have an office and you have hallways that tends to happen. Now in this remote world, you need to intentionally recruit for that. Who are the people that can bring that energy?

Roy: Has that changed your hiring process? Is there explicit scoring of the "remote readiness" of a candidate?

Angela: It's not part of an official scoring. Maybe it should be. It's definitely something we take into account right now [during the pandemic]. iRobot does have a hardware component to it. There are physical robots and we do need physical real estate to test them, so I suspect that we'll always be headquarter adjacent. But it is something that we look at right now. Is this somebody, who, starting out, not having the hallways, will be able to just pop meetings onto people's calendars and help themselves gain context?

Roy: In the current situation do you have an explicit process for new, remote hires to get to know all the people on the team?

Angela: There's the official onboarding period, where you learn about benefits and that stuff. And then there is the team-based onboarding, which is the one that we define. We have a schedule of the people that you need to meet, the contacts, the location of the wikis and everything, so that you can learn on your own. Also we have a schedule of checkpoint meetings to monitor progress. Skip-level meetings, etc. New hire's will have a 30/60/90 day plan, with the 30 being very detailed and the others becoming less granular.

Roy: Let's say you have a new hire coming onboard. Do you do any special prep for the team itself? Anything remote specific?

Angela: We've had such crazy, explosive growth, that there are just constantly new people. So we don't really prepare the team, since there's always new people to onboard. It feels like two new people every week.

As far as remote, we are currently hiring remote, but it's not clear how it will work long-term, whether we hire people away from one of our offices.

Roy: Thanks so much for talking to me today.

Angela: Thank you. Please have everyone check out our careers page at iRobot. We're hiring!

Chapter 6: Technical skills assessment

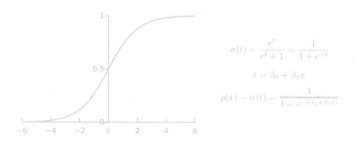

Once you have started to collect applications and decided on your overall selection strategy, you need to get into the details of how you will assess those candidates for both technical and professional skills. In this chapter we will cover strategies for assessing the technical skills that are core to the work of data scientists and machine learning engineers.

We'll start off discussing technical skills assessment strategies, then cover specific skills and how to assess them. Chapter 7 will cover how to design and conduct interviews to help you best decide which candidates you should be making job offers to.

Skills assessment

Data science and machine learning are about doing. In order to know if your job candidates can successfully perform in the role you are seeking to fill, you need to better understand if they can do the tasks that will be part of that role. In other words, you need to assess their current skills.

What does it mean to assess technical skills?

Assessing technical skills is an accepted part of interviews for data science and software engineering roles today. It's a good exercise to step back and ask yourself what skills assessment really means and why it's done in the first place.

Your new hire needs to be able to execute the tasks that they are hired to perform. How will you know that they are able to execute those tasks before you actually hire them? This is a simple question, but as you'll see in the rest of this chapter, the answer is not necessarily straight forward.

As I will mention repeatedly in this chapter, skills assessment is a controversial topic. No matter the approach or strategy, you will find vocal critics. One question you might have is "why do we even bother?". Many highly skilled professions do not have anything like a technical assessment. A surgeon, for example, is not asked to demonstrate an appendectomy as part of their interview process. In contrast to a field like medicine, data science and ML engineering are not regulated professions with skills and training certifications, licenses, or limits on who can become one. Unlike professions such as medicine or law, anyone can claim to be a data scientist[30] and apply to work for you. Not only that, but the field is very broad and a lot of the definitions of the terminology are not widely agreed upon. That means that even a data scientist or machine learning engineer with experience may not have the specific skills your role needs. Ultimately this means that some form of skills assessment is something almost all employers opt for in their hiring process.

Given that skills assessment is something you'll likely want to do,

---

[30]I personally think the lack of gatekeeping is a good thing for the profession, even if it makes our lives as hiring managers more difficult. Lack of regulation here opens the doors to a much broader set of people. Also the extremely fast pace of change in these fields would make certification and regulation very difficult to do well, at best.

it's unfortunately not as simple as determining if a candidate can do the tasks of the role. For one thing, it's typically unlikely that you can have a candidate actually perform the real work that they would be doing in the role as part of your assessment process[31]. Time and learning barriers to your specific tasks tend to make that untenable. Instead, the most common approach is to assess the candidate on proxy tasks that are similar in the general flavor of the tasks that they would perform as employees.

Another common question related to assessments is whether it's possible to simply hire smart people and teach them or let them learn the needed tasks on the job. This is possible in certain roles[32], though typically your candidates need to have an adequate level of foundational skills to be successful in a reasonable time frame. For example, programming is the type of skill that will take a fair amount of time for someone to go from zero to productive. If you have a large organization with a lot of resources, training people into a role might be possible, but you still need some way to assess the candidate's potential to learn and perform the tasks for your role. This effectively puts you back to square one.

Another common question is whether it is even possible to assess technical skills in an effective, consistent way. Can you formulate an assessment that is objective and reflects a candidate's true skill level, rather than just their ability to do well on an assessment test? Will candidates simply study or memorize common assessment questions? These are all reasonable questions and it's not clear that you can both achieve the former goals and avoid the latter completely. In the rest of the chapter we will examine several approaches and discuss the pros, cons, and tradeoffs.

---

[31]Some companies, such as Automattic, actually do have hiring processes where the candidate will work along side the employees in a sort of paid trial process for a period of time. These can be part-time or full-time trials. While they give the company and the candidate a better sense of each other, there are obviously a lot of limiting factors in play that make this approach not possible for every company and every candidate.

[32]Effectively this is what happens in all roles, but how much a new employee needs to learn is the big question. Even an expert will need to learn the specifics of your tools, infrastructure, team, and business. This is very different from not knowing the foundational skills of the role, though.

How can you assess technical skills?

There are many approaches to assessing technical skills and no single formula that is best in every situation. As previously mentioned, strong opinions about how (or if) skills assessments should be done are ubiquitous. It's common to see organizations making up things from scratch or wholesale copying what other, seemingly successful organizations are doing. This is often done without a lot of consideration regarding how well that will fit their own needs or why the other company landed on that solution.

In this section we'll examine several approaches to technical skills assessment with the goal of helping you make a more informed decision on the best strategy for hiring data scientists and ML engineers in your organization.

What are we trying to assess?

We will start with the question of what types of technical skills we are trying to assess. As mentioned in previous chapters, there is a large list of skills that are associated with different tasks and roles. Some of the most common skills for data-centric roles are:

- Programming (in a specific language)
- Statistics and probability knowledge
- Data exploration and visualization skills
- Data extraction, manipulation, and cleaning
- Machine learning methods
- Common tools for ML, data pipelines, statistical analysis, etc
- Common software development practices
- Systems design

In a subsequent section we will discuss which specific skills to assess, but here we want to consider which of these can be reasonably assessed and how.

Computer programming is probably the most commonly assessed technical skill of the categories listed above (and possibly the one to draw the most controversy). An important question to ask yourself is what exactly you want to know about a candidate's programming skills.

- Are they able to write basic programs?
- Can they program in a specific paradigm, such as functional programming?
- Can they use a specific language?
- Are they fluent in the use of a specific framework or library?
- Are they able to write efficient or high performance code?
- Do they use "best practices" in their code?
- Are they familiar with standard algorithms and data structures?
- Do they know the specific tricks to solve certain programming puzzles?

What you want to assess will depend on the needs and circumstances of your open role, team, and situation. You may need someone fluent in a specific framework immediately. On the other hand, you may use something uncommon or simply have the time to teach new hires how to use your particular programming stack.

For all of the skills listed previously, exactly what aspects of them you want to assess will depend on the your resources and constraints. In more general terms, you need to decide, where you are on a spectrum from a candidate needing general, generic skills to very specific skills, with the latter being typically harder to find (or afford). This will inform how you design the content of your assessments.

Methods for skills assessment

Beyond deciding what you should be assessing, you need to decide how you will actually perform the assessment. While your overall goals should be to have an effective, fair, and efficient assessment, there are several possible methods to choose from, including:

- Take-home assessments
- Online quizzes
- Live pair programming
- Having a candidate present prior (typically open source) code they have written
- Sourcing from a service that pre-vets skills

Each of these methods and how they're used has some pros and cons, which we will examine. These are also part of the heart of much controversy around skills assessment techniques.

Take home assessments: A take-home assessment is simply assessment material that a candidate will work on in their own time in the place of their choosing (typically "at home"). For DS and MLE, this could be a set of questions related to a data set, a programming task, a task to build an ML model, or several other options. Typically a candidate is given a deadline ranging from hours to days from when the material becomes available.

Take home assessments can be very flexible with regards to when the candidate can actually work on them, what they can cover, and the format. Instead of a quiz-style assessment, the take home can be more like a project or other form of work. Candidates are able to use their own "home" computing tools and environments.

Common objections to take homes are that they favor some groups over others, e.g. people who don't currently have full-time work may have more time to work on these, while people with full-time work and family-related duties may have very little time. There is also concern for cheating, when a candidate can spend so much time with the material, or simply give it to others easily. Finally, a longer, potentially open-ended assessment presents a challenge for scoring, either because there is simply a lot of material or because the material may differ so much from one candidate to the next. The logistics of coordinating sending the materials out at a specific time and enforcing deadlines can also present problems.

Online quizzes: Online quizzes are assessment materials that is hosted online. This can be self-hosted, but is more typically done using a third party skills assessment platform. This is most common for programming skills assessment, but there is a growing amount of material available related to other DS and MLE skills. Many commercial platforms will provide entire assessments or individual questions or tasks for you to choose for your assessment. Some will allow you to use your own assessment questions and tasks. Many platforms will record the candidate's typing, allowing the person scoring or assessing the work to view how the candidate entered their work. In addition to the video playback of typing, some platforms have algorithms that try to detect plagiarism, with varying degrees of success.

Online quizzes allow you to relatively easily send assessments to many candidates, since the services are often integrated with applicant tracking systems or allow you to send out assessments from a website on demand. If you use off-the-shelf assessment questions, they are typically scored automatically by the service and often are accompanied by statistics related to how the candidate performed relative to others (potentially beyond your candidate pool). Typically these platforms will allow a candidate to take the quiz whenever they can within some time window, while restricting the total time that the candidate works on the quiz (e.g. a candidate my be able to click the link any time in the next two weeks and then will have 90 minutes to complete the assessment once they start).

Online quizzes have several potential drawbacks. If you are using a commercial assessment platform the costs may be high. If you self-host, the time and resources needed to maintain the online quiz may be prohibitive. Another aspect is that you may not have as much control over the material as you'd prefer, depending on the platform. Many of the skills assessment platforms use questions that have been widely circulated and solutions to those questions are easily available, leading to plagiarism.

Live pair programming: Live pair programming is a type of skills assessment interview where a candidate and an interviewer both use the same platform to interactively work on a problem together. Typically the interviewer will pose the task or question to the candidate and then offer help or hints along the way. Both interviewer and candidate can see and type on the live programming platform. There are several commercial platforms that enable this. Some organizations even use tools like Google Docs for this purpose, though this is usually recounted with horror by candidates.

The benefits include getting a live view into how someone works on a problem, allowing the candidate to easily ask questions, and being able to provide real-time hints and assistance. Additionally, you can tailor the problem to the candidate's skill level as you go. Live pair programming can be done either in person or online.

Drawbacks to live pair programming include those common to all live interviewing formats: difficulty scaling the process, the added difficulty of scheduling all parties, candidates' anxiety interacting with the interviewers, and variation between and among interviewers. Additionally, the candidate is typically using an environment that is different than the one they would typically use for "real" work. The costs associated with live pair programming platforms may be high.

Presenting prior work: Presenting prior work is a skills assessment technique, where the candidate will present something that they had previously worked on in a professional, educational, or hobby setting. The idea is to have the candidate walk the interviewer through an example of strong work that they have done, explaining decisions they made, and demonstrating their expertise. This can be in the form of a code walk through, a write up, or a presentation.

The advantages of having the candidate present prior work include getting a view into how they perform "real world" work, rather than a relatively contrived assessment problem, having the candidate speak about something they know in depth, and allowing the interviewer to better assess the candidate's technical communication skills.

One of the main drawbacks with presenting prior work is scoring the assessment in a consistent way, due to the inherent variation in the material. Another issue is that some candidates may have little or no access to previous work they've done for logistical or legal reasons. This may result in them having to present work from long ago in the past or on something that is much less substantial than other candidates are able to present. This is also a type of assessment that is inherently difficult to scale.

Sourcing from a third party: Another option is to have a third party that does its own technical screening process suggest candidates to you. Typically these services screen large numbers of candidates for common technical skills and then charge employers a finders fee if the candidate is successfully placed. Most of these services are aimed at software developers, but there is a growing number aimed at data scientist and MLE placement.

The primary advantages of such services are that it removes some of the screening burden from the employer and potentially gives you a better understanding of how a candidate's skills compare to a large population of peers.

These services are not typically cheap. Additionally, you have no control over the assessment material or format that's being used. You will have to trust what the service is doing. Some employers use these services as an extra filter in front of their established process. While this may help reduce false positives in the interview process, the question of return on investment is still something that the employer will need to consider.

Creating a fair skills assessment

There are several reasons why creating a fair skills assessment should be one of your goals. Besides the fact that you want as unbiased an understanding of your candidates' skills as possible to aid your decision making, fairness is the right thing to do.

To create a fair assessment, you want to remove potential sources of bias and reduce the chance of cheating. Reducing bias means that you want to create as uniform a process as possible, while allowing for certain accommodations. Means for reducing bias include:

- Using automated scoring on problems with unambiguous answers.
- Creating and sticking to scoring rubrics for more open-ended or subjective problems.
- Training team members on how to administer and score assessments.
- Having multiple people administer and score assessments.
- Randomly selecting assessment questions / tasks from an approved pool of tasks, rather than letting team members choose.

In order to reduce cheating, you need to have a large pool of possible questions and tasks to choose from and ideally cycle out older questions and introduce brand new questions on a regular basis. This will not eliminate cheating, but can reduce it somewhat. For detecting cheating, some platforms have built-in plagiarism detection, with varying levels of accuracy. It is also good practice to have a technical session when you do live interviews that serves in part as a double check. This has proven useful in my experience.

You will have cheaters

When you give a test-like skills assessment, you will inevitably have cheaters. If you are using common or known questions, some candidates will search for solutions online and copy-paste or slightly modify what they find, sometimes with breath-taking boldness and sloppiness. Other times, candidates will get help directly from another person.

I have seen this in many forms, including candidates that clearly had someone else help them create their submission for open-ended takehomes and candidates that submitted nearly identical solutions only seconds apart from one another.

I even once contacted the director of a graduate program to let them know that a very high number of applicants from their program had all cheated on our skills assessment. The director was saddened and horrified.

It's very frustrating, but a zero tolerance policy is probably the only way to go. To be as fair as possible, you should be very explicit about what is and is not allowed on your assessment.

Deciding on your strategy

To decide which method you will use to conduct your technical skills assessment, you need to account for your candidate volume, your resources, and time constraints. Additionally you should consider some logistical facets, such as the need to integrate with your applicant tracking or scheduling systems.

The big question then comes down to where on the "build versus buy" spectrum you want to be. You should lay out all of these options and try to constrain them against your financial and time budgets. Keep in mind that all choices will require some level of maintenance. I suggest that you try out different systems if possible, before making a final choice.

Other miscellaneous considerations to keep in mind:

- Who needs to be able to access the assessments?
- Where will the scores live? A spreadsheet? The ATS?
- Do you need to create dedicated interviewing / scoring time from your teammates?
- Do you need tight integration with existing systems (e.g. the ATS)?
- What level of human interaction can you budget for?
  - I.e. for scheduling, proctoring, scoring, etc
  - How automated does this all need to be?
- How important is it that you control the material?
  - Are you OK with off-the-shelf questions / tasks?

Which skills should you be assessing?

Once you have decided *how* you are going to administer your technical skills assessment, there is the decision to make around which specific skills you will be assessing.

Referring back to Chapter 3 on defining roles and Appendices I and II, you can get an idea of which skills you will want to assess for the roles you are hiring. There are too many skills to test all of the relevant skills in detail for any given role. It's best to choose the highest level version of skills (e.g. basic Python programming) and a few of the most important skills specific to the role (e.g. time series forecasting). Typically, testing knowledge of specific tools is not a super strong signal, as you can train a new hire on specific tools, though this is not without trade-offs (or controversy).

For a generalist data science position, I have focussed on establishing a candidate's ability to do basic data handling and analysis, basic programming in the language of the team, and basic ML skills as the focus of the initial technical skills assessment.

Should everyone get the same assessment?

Does one size fit all when assessing technical skills? So far we've been looking at a pretty generic way to assess skills without really talking about the fact that you might have several roles that vary greatly in scope or seniority. For example, you may be trying to hire interns and a new director of machine learning at the same time. Does everyone just get sent the same link to an online quiz?

As you might suspect, the answer is generally "no". There are multiple reasons for this. One obvious reason is that different roles require different skills and different skill levels. In addition, for different roles, e.g. junior versus senior, your applicant pools will be very different in size. This means that you can and may need to deal with each applicant in different ways (i.e. spend more or less time per candidate). Also, the technical skills of a candidate may have very different weights by role. For example, a manager should have a strong grasp on the technical aspects of DS or MLE, but their primary skill set is around people and project management and strategy.

That all said, sometimes you will give roles of different seniorities the same assessment, but often at different times in the interview process and / or with different scoring criteria or passing thresholds.

Choosing assessment material

Once you have decided on how you are going to conduct the technical skills assessment and what skills you want to cover, you need to decide on specific assessment material.

As mentioned previously, your options range from designing your own assessment material from scratch to using an assessment completely designed by a third party. We will briefly discuss some of the advantages and disadvantages of approaches on this spectrum.

Making your own: By making your own assessment material, you are assured full control over the material. You can tailor the assessment to the very specific skills of your role, set the scoring criteria, and weigh the resulting scores as most appropriate for your needs. Fundamentally this the most flexible approach.

The down side of making your own assessment material includes the amount of effort in creating material from scratch, assessing the material itself[33], designing the scoring criteria, relative score weights, and maintaining the pool of material over time. You also need to use an assessment infrastructure that will accommodate your material[34], which may need substantial effort or resources to implement. All of the above has a cost in time spent by your team and others.

Using third party material: Using assessment material created by a third party is convenient. Clearly there is a time savings in the actual creation of the material. Additionally, it's possible that the people authoring the material have the experience and data to create stronger material than you and your team could create

---

[33]It's a good idea to have several people try out the assessment material to look for issues and gauge the appropriateness of the material. It is surprisingly easy to mis-calibrate the difficulty of assessment material. You'll be equally unhappy when all of your candidates can easily do the assessment or when no one is able to do it. Ideally you want material that produces a (meaningful) distribution of scores.

[34]The "infrastructure" you use for administering your assessment could be as simple as sending an email or as complicated as building your own testing platform that integrates into your other hiring systems.

on your own. Also, it's likely that a third party will have a larger amount of assessment material than your team would reasonably create. In the best case scenario, the third party may have prepared assessments that are well tested and well suited to your hiring needs.

On the other hand, you will still need to convince yourself that the assessment material from the third party is high quality. Some services simply collect known material from the web and other sources, with little effort put into vetting the material. This ends up inviting cheating on online assessments, as candidates will search for these questions and find them. Others may have a reasonable assessment, but it will simply not meet your specific needs. Additionally there will be a monetary cost to using the service.

You may find yourself somewhere in the middle, using a mix of material provided by a third party and custom material that you and your team have created. This is not inherently better than either of the other approaches, but may be the most convenient choice, depending on your specific constraints.

Assessing your assessment material

Once you've chosen or created your material, you'll need to assess the quality of it. The point of a skills assessment it give you useful information to select the best candidates for your role. High quality skills assessment material needs to meet a few objectives:

1. Test skills that are relevant to the role.
2. Have a difficulty level that results in a distribution of scores.
3. Be unique enough, such that cheating is not easy, but generic enough to test foundational skills rather than knowledge of tricks.

Should you use fizzbuzz?

In the world of technical skills assessments for computer programmers there is a famous (infamous?) screening problem called *fizzbuzz*. The idea is that fizzbuzz is easy enough such that any minimally competent programmer should be able to solve it. Additionally, stories abound of candidates with long, impressive looking resumes, who have somehow managed to make it that far in their careers without the skills to solve something as simple as fizzbuzz. The idea behind fizzbuzz is to quickly screen those candidates out that look good on paper, but don't have the basic skills needed for the role.

Fizzbuzz is just one example, but there is a broader question about whether you should give *easy* questions to candidates. Some candidates may find easy questions insulting, but a more substantive argument against easy questions is that you would give a strong candidate more difficult questions anyway, so why not start with more difficult questions. Someone who can't solve fizzbuzz surely can't do linked list gymnastics or invert a binary tree!

I think that fizzbuzz can have a place though. If you have an early stage, where you do a quick screen of the candidate (it could even be part of the application), fizzbuzz and similar very easy problems can be useful early filters. This can help avoid wasting both the candidate's and your team's time. Otherwise I tend to agree that super easy problems probably don't have much utility in the skills assessment process.

So how do you actually assess your assessment materials? You need to get people to take it. I suggest that you first have members of your team try completing the problems/tasks (assuming they did not create the material themselves). At this point you want feedback to see if the instructions make sense, if the material is reasonable in difficulty, and on the appropriateness of the material for the role.

> ## "I doubt I could pass our tech screen"
>
> One comment that you often hear from members of tech teams is that they feel that the (new) tech screen being used by the team is too hard and that they wouldn't be able to pass it. In my experience, this tends to be mostly an expression of self-doubt on the part of your team members.
>
> It's important to get good critical feedback on your assessment material from knowledgeable people. If your team members express reservations, make it clear to them that you will keep individual results of the team private and that your focus is getting specific, useful feedback. If the assessment material is truly too difficult, your goal is to adjust it to the right level, not to re-assess your team members' skills.

If everyone on your team is getting everything right in less than the time allotted, the material is probably too easy. If most are struggling and not finishing, the material is probably too difficult. You want to be somewhere in the middle. In a subsequent section we'll talk about re-assessing the material once you've started having actual candidates take your assessment.

Scoring and decision making

Once you have decided on your technical skills assessment material and refined it through feedback, you need to come up with a way to score a candidate's performance and subsequently make decisions.

Scoring

When scoring candidates' solutions, the goal is to quantify their performances both accurately and consistently. For highly specified problems, there may simply be correct (or "working") solutions and incorrect solutions, making your job easy (e.g. multiple choice questions, numerical answers, code that passes the tests). For more open ended problems, using a rubric and training the people scoring on how to use the rubric is the best strategy to achieve accuracy and consistency. Additional measures to reduce bias can be to remove the information that identifies the candidate and having more than one person score the assessment of each candidate.

To create a rubric you should try to determine the specific goals of the assessment problem, break those into categories, and assign point values for different levels of completeness or goodness. For example, in evaluating the code a candidate submitted for a specific problem, you might assign various amounts of points for

- The code running without error.
- The legibility of the code.
- The style of the code (i.e. does it follow the expected or common conventions of the language).
- The efficiency of the code when running.
- Overall impression of the solution.

Some criteria may be binary (e.g. whether the code ran without error), while other maybe more subjective (e.g. overall impression). Because of this, it's important for there to be instruction to the scorers on how to apply the rubric.

At this point you should have a process that will provide a numerical score that hopefully reflects how a candidate has performed on the assessment, but you must also decide the relative importance of each component, question, or task on you assessment. In other words, you will need to decided how each item is weighted for the overall score.

Scoring may be something that is built into your assessment software or may need to be tracked separately. A (shared) spreadsheet is often sufficient, though you may want to also keep scores in your ATS.

Decision making

Once you have a scoring procedure in place, you will want to decide on your decision process. For technical assessments used as a standalone screen, the decision process often comes down to a score threshold.

A score threshold should ideally achieve two things: identifying candidates above a minimum needed skill level and narrowing the funnel to your maximum pipeline capacity for the next stage. Setting this threshold is difficult to do a priori, which presents a dilemma: how do you handle the first set of candidates that take your skills assessment? I think there are two reasonable options:

1. Make a best guess of the threshold and move candidates that score above the threshold to the next stage, noting that this was based on the initial threshold.
2. Delay setting the threshold until you have enough candidates to make a more informed guess.

The first strategy allows you to immediately move candidates forward, but at the risk of promoting or rejecting people you didn't want to promote or reject. The second strategy lets you gather some data first to better set a threshold, but at the risk of delaying candidates in your process for too long.

The life cycle of your assessments

As with the overall hiring process, your technical skills assessment will ultimately be a living, evolving thing. In this section we'll discuss how the material will typically change over time.

Some questions won't be very good: Just as saying "no plan survives contact with the enemy"[35], no assessment survives contact with candidates unscathed. Even after having gotten feedback from knowledgeable people (e.g. your team members) will find that some questions are simply too easy, too hard, or just not suitable in some way.

There will be cheating: You are likely to discover that some of your candidates are cheating in some way on your assessments. There are many ways to cheat, but the most common ones are searching for existing answers to the questions online or having someone else help them (for online assessments). In person assessments are much less likely to have cheating, though it's not unheard of. To reduce the chances of cheating, you should first be very explicit about what is and what's not allowed. Using material that is original will reduce the chance people can simply do a web search and find existing answers online, but is not foolproof. Even with a brand new assessment, the more candidates that take your assessment, the greater the chance that the material will be posted online. Refreshing your material regularly is the best way to deal with this. You cannot eliminate cheating, but one way to help reinforce the signal you're getting is to have more than one round of technical assessment (e.g. an early online assessment and an "onsite" assessment in the final rounds).

Needed skills will change: Over time you may find that the skills that your roles need will change. This means you will need to reevaluate the suitability of your material or relative weights and adjust accordingly.

---

[35]Attributed to Moltke the Elder.

Thresholds will change: You may find that over time the performance of candidates on your assessment changes. Assuming that the change is not due to cheating, e.g. you have found a different population of candidates, you may need to adjust your decision thresholds.

Scaling: If you see a significant increase in your candidate pool, your initial process may no longer be able to meet the time and resource constraints that you have. You may need to design a whole new assessment process at this point.

For most of these issues, keeping an eye on key metrics will help to alert you early and help you diagnose issues. Some metrics you may want to track include:

- Distribution of scores
- Pass / fail rate
- Cheating frequency (if possible)
- Similar metrics on individual problems / tasks

Considerations for "live" skills assessments

Much of the above is applicable to both online and live skills assessments, but in this sections we'll discuss some specific issues and considerations for live assessments, whether in person or over the internet. Unlike online assessments, live assessments typically involve an interviewer being present, though some hiring teams will leave candidates in a room on their own to work on the assessment.

For live assessments the interviewer may have several potential duties, including:

- Explaining the instructions

- Answering questions
- Offering hints
- Observing the candidate's behavior
- Contributing to the solution, a la pair programming

Performing these duties in a way that is consistent and fair can be more difficult than simply scoring an assessment. It's important that you create explicit instructions and training for the interviewers. Without very clear expectations, it's easy for candidates to receive very different levels of assistance, for example. Your interviewing instructions may include how to present the material to the candidate, how and to what extent the interviewer can assist the candidate, what to take notes on, etc.

Summary

The most important take-aways in this chapter are:

- Skills assessment is both controversial and unsolved.
- The most you can do is to make your best attempt by understanding the pros and cons of different approaches.
- Strive for fairness, robustness, and efficiency in the assessment.
- You need to consider all of the resources and constraints you have and design a skills assessment process that will best meet your goals.
- Automate as much as you can.
- Use a scoring rubric and train people on how to apply it.
- You will need to adapt your process along the way to match scale issues, cheating, shifting needs in the roles, and other unforeseen issues.

Interview: Ravi Mody, Spotify

Ravi Mody is an Engineering Manager at Spotify, where he leads a team of machine learning engineers working on recommendations. He previously held leadership positions at Daily Harvest, Boxed, and iHeartRadio. Prior to working in data science, Ravi studied electrical engineering and computer science.

Ravi can be found on Twitter @ravi_mody[a].

In the interview below, Ravi discusses some of the main challenges faced by machine learning hiring managers and some of the approaches that he has used to address those challenges.

---

[a]https://twitter.com/ravi_mody

Roy: Hi Ravi. Thank you for talking to me today. Let's start off by having you introduce yourself and tell us a little bit about your background related to data science and machine learning.

Ravi: Thanks so much for having me. My background is in machine learning and data, but if you zoom way back I've been programming since I was ten years old. I found QBasic one time and I really fell in love with the fact that I could tell a computer what to do. In high school I started getting into real languages like C++. I wrote a Connect Four program. It was probably the most embarrassing code I've ever written, but when I ran it, it actually beat me! It was one of the best feelings that I ever had. Even almost thirty years later it feels like one of the coolest things I've ever done. Ever since then I've been on the path to teach computers to do stuff.

Roy: Very cool.

Ravi: That led me to doing robotics as an undergrad. I studied electrical engineering and computer engineering. It was great, but it wasn't really clear what I would do. So I decided to do a masters in computer science at UCSD[36]. As an undergrad I also did some computer vision research.

Roy: This was back in the pre-data science days, when people pursued machine learning and computer vision because they thought it was cool and that was it? Not because of the big bucks?

Ravi: Yeah. We were nerds who wanted to do math in our free time.

Roy: Tell us about your career path going from a newbie to a seasoned manager?

Ravi: Out of grad school, my first job was at FICO. You may know them because they do FICO scores, credit scoring. The team that I joined was actually doing credit card fraud detection. When you use your card, usually FICO is the one running a fraud detection algorithm. It's a neural network that decides if it's fraud. I was really lucky to get a job there, because it really ramped up my machine learning knowledge. How you do big data machine learning. Again, this was before data science was really a thing. Back then the explosion of data hadn't really happened yet in most industries.

I wanted to move back to the East Coast and I joined an adtech company. That was around the time that the term "data science" was invented. It was a revelation to me. It's when I realized that the MBA's in suits actually cared about data. That's also where I learned to be professional and some of the softer skills. When you talk and you're a data person, people would actually listen to you. You can back what you're saying with data.

---

[36]University of California, San Diego

Next I joined iHeartRadio to do machine learning. I joined at a time when there was a lot of data, but not yet ML. All heuristics and rule-based stuff. I started doing some research and learning more about these machine learning methods that could really simplify a lot of what we were doing and make it better. I presented that vision to senior leadership and they asked me to start building the machine learning and data science team there. I got really lucky at the time. They wanted to show that they were serious about this, so they promoted me to Director of Data Science. This gave me the opportunity to learn how to build teams, how to hire people, how to manage the business side of a data team. I spent a couple years there and had a ton of fun.

Next I went to Boxed, a smaller company, because I wanted to get experience around setting strategy. I was VP of Data Science there and sat on the leadership team. In addition to building the team and doing data science, I was able be part of the leadership meetings and understand the direction that the company was going in. That helped me better direct the data science team in the same direction and I gained more leadership chops.

After Boxed I joined Daily Harvest, where I joined as VP of Data, taking over analytics and building out a data engineering team and a data products / machine learning team. And then I joined Spotify as an Engineering Manager.

Roy: What are you doing at Spotify?

Ravi: At Spotify I manage the team that does music discovery. Our mission is to connect our listeners with new types of music. The team is primarily a mix of data engineers, backend engineers, and machine learning engineers.

Roy: Over the course of your career, what kind of roles have you hired?

Ravi: I've mostly hired machine learning people. Between Boxed and Daily Harvest, I got more involved with analytics hiring, as well as data engineering hiring.

Roy: What do you see as the biggest challenge in hiring data people?

Ravi: I think one of the most challenging things is finding really strong machine learning practitioners who also really understand the business value. One of the big challenges is that often times PM's[37] do not clearly understand the full value of machine learning. So you really want to depend on your machine learning engineers to help them understand and deliver the value to the company. It's often a "unicorn". Someone who is an excellent machine learning engineer and also has a lot of empathy for what senior leadership at a company is thinking about, what the product managers are thinking about, what really needs to be built.

Roy: Would you say those are typically going to be more experienced people?

Ravi: Typically yes, but experience does not necessarily buy you that kind of intuition. Ultimately there are people who don't have any interest in the business side. There are some people who it just doesn't resonate that much with.

Another thing is that machine learning evolves very quickly. That introduces two challenges: one is that a lot of new MLE's skip over the basics. I've talked to people who say, "I've built these deep neural networks, but what the hell is logistic regression??". The other side is that you have people who've been doing machine learning for years, but they're not keeping up with all of the new stuff. So finding people with that breadth of ML knowledge can be a real challenge.

Roy: That's definitely a challenge. I've seen both of those issues.

What changes have you noticed in hiring?

Ravi: One of the big changes is that there are more and more people who have experience, but there are far, far more people entering the industry who have no experience. It's created some really interesting supply and demand dynamics. A clear trend is that more

---

[37]Product managers

and more businesses are saying "we need machine learning people". What's great is that there are now people that have five years of experience. Back in 2012 it was a little absurd to ask for people with five years of experience. Today you can find those people, but they tend to get paid very well and to be in high demand.

For any job I've put up for machine learning engineers in the last couple years I've had something like 500 applicants. Every resume looks the same. They don't have experience. They come out of a boot camp. Every boot camp kind of builds up the same resume. That's a challenge. I want to give those people opportunities. I don't just want to hire people with five years experience, but it can be tricky wading through all of those resumes.

Another newer trend I've seen in data science is the bifurcation of analytics and machine learning is becoming much bigger. When I got my first data science title in, I think, 2011 or 2012, the two were completely linked. If you were a data scientist you had to know machine learning. You had to know analytics. You had to be in that little Venn diagram. But I think today that Venn diagram has been starting to separate. And I actually see that as largely a good thing. The machine learning engineers are starting to become true software engineers. You need to know git really well. You need to know testing. MLE's are increasingly expected to be building really high quality software. Whereas analysts are increasingly just expected to understand the business really well. In my experience, very few people are really good at both of those things.

Roy: What have you seen as the difference between hiring at large companies and smaller companies and also hiring at tech companies versus more traditional companies?

Ravi: At smaller companies, especially if there are only a couple teams, the hiring manager is really building the reputation of the team. You don't get that for free, like you do at a bigger company. The brand often will not carry itself. So it's up to the manager to spend a lot of their time reaching out to people and actually building out the funnel. Somebody who's interested in your company can't just search for "Small Company data science" and get a lot of info, unless you actually go out and do something about that. I've found that giving talks and writing blog posts is really helpful. Pretty much anytime I've done something like that, the number of candidates drastically increases.

At a big company you don't need to do that. Nobody's wondering "Oh, I wonder what it's like to work at Facebook?" or if they are, they can do a search for "Facebook data science" and probably find 50 articles about that. So it's up to the hiring manager at a smaller company to really build out that brand.

Setting up the interview process is also really important. Usually at a smaller company you're not going to have a recruiter that's devoted to data science and machine learning. They will often really depend on you to put those processes in place and explain to them what's valuable and what's not. At a big company you may have a recruiter specifically devoted to a headcount of thirty to fifty in data science and machine learning. The process is generally a lot more standardized. I'd say the challenge there is keeping the standardization, which is really valuable. In a big tech company you really want to make sure that the process is standard across all of the people that you're interviewing. At a smaller company you can give a lot more attention to specific candidates and make a more "surgical" hire. You're only hiring one or two people and the wrong hire may destroy your team.

Roy: What strategies or processes do you recommend managers use to help get the right people on their teams?

Ravi: I'm a big fan of the take-home. I know this can be somewhat controversial, but I think what's really great about the take-home is that it gives people the chance to work in the environment that they're really comfortable with. They have their computer. They have their text editor or IDE. They can look at things online. It really impersonates what it would actually be like to work at the job. It's often a way of actually selling the job. You make the take home kind of fun and give them actual data.

Roy: At what step in the hiring process do you give people that take-home? And how do you scale that?

Ravi: That's a great question. I used to give the take-home to anyone who wanted it. I would use it as like a screen. If you want to spend your time being screened, that's great. What I found was that I was actually wasting a lot of people's time. I could take a look at their resume and immediately say "sure you could do fine on the take home, but there's no chance you have the experience to be successful at this job".

One of the things I'm very sensitive about is that take-homes are inherently somewhat unfair. We're taking people's time. We're not paying them for it, usually. It can create a pretty big power imbalance. I can go through ten take-homes in like an hour and that represents like a hundred hours of people's time. So I started doing some resume screening before I sent out the take-home. My general idea is that I want them to have at least a 10% - 20% chance of passing the technical portions after the take-home.

Roy: How screened are the candidates before you see their resumes?

Ravi: That's highly dependent on the company and whether the recruiters are doing resume screens. I've done both. I've had recruiters do screening and I've done screening. I've definitely gone into a pile of 500 resumes digitally and had to spend like six hours going through all of them. Sometimes I'll have a recruiter filter out 95% of them for me. But I'll usually be the one making the call about who gets the take-home.

Roy: A slightly random question: when you are hiring candidates? Do you rely on background checks as part of the process and how important is that?

Ravi: I have never conducted one. I don't even do reference calls, because I don't trust them. I'm not sure that I've ever worked at a company that does them, except maybe when I was working in finance.

Roy: That's the kind of thing that candidates ask about, but I'm not even sure that anyone's ever run a background check on me or asked for references in my tech career. I think it's one of those differences between tech companies and "traditional" companies.

Ravi: I've fielded some reference calls for people that listed me as a reference, but even then it didn't seem like the companies were placing much weight on it.

Roy: Once you've found the right person and they've accepted an offer, what are the things that you think are good or crucial for setting them up for success?

Ravi: I love that question, by the way, because I think it's something that every manager needs to think a lot about. When you ask a lot of people why they left a job, it's either "I don't think my manager has my back" or "I'm not continuing to grow". It's on the manager to make sure people are happy.

One of the things I often tell my team is that I want to help them create awesome bullet points on their resumes for their next job. Part of that is understanding their strengths and interests and then aligning that with the business. What I'll usually do when somebody starts is sit down with them and write a typical 30/60/90 day plan, but I'll also ask "where do you see yourself in two to five years?" It's really important to me that that person continues to develop themself in that direction. It tends to make for really happy employees.

At any given point, everyone on the team should be either learning something new or doing something that's going to have an impact. That's what's ultimately going to make those bullet points. It's either "this is what I learned" or "I did this and this is the impact it had". As long as they're adding bullet points, they'll probably stay at the job. That's how you create a team that stays together.

Roy: Thank you very much Ravi. It was really good to hear your perspective and about your diverse work experience feeding into that perspective.

Ravi: Thanks for having me.

Chapter 7: Interviewing

$$P(A|B) = \frac{P(B|A)P(A)}{P(B)}$$

We have covered how to design and conduct technical skills assessments, but the technical skills assessment is only one part of the full interviewing strategy. Data scientists and MLE's have not only specialized skill sets, but they play specific roles on their teams. The goal of interviewing is to determine whether a candidate has the technical and non-technical skills for the role, as well as their overall "fit" for the role and their potential for growth.

In this chapter we will discuss why and how to design and conduct the holistic interviews used to determine if a candidate is right for the role and your team.

The goals of the interview process

Once you have done your initial selection of applicants, whether via a first stage technical screen or a resume screen, the remaining interviews are aimed at achieving several goals:

- Gaining a more complete understanding of the candidate's technical skills and potential, relative to the role.
- Gaining a more complete understanding of the candidate's experience working in similar environments (i.e. team work, subject matter, remote, etc).
- Gaining an understanding of how the candidate would fit on the current team and and with future plans for the team.

- Gaining an understanding of the candidate's goals and expectations.

Overall you are looking for indications that the candidate can successfully execute (or quickly learn to execute) the tasks of the role, positively contribute to the team and the wider company, and ultimately add value. Within the framework of your overall hiring and interviewing strategy, you want to maximize the information you get on the candidate, while balancing the interviews against your constraints, but also making the process as reasonable for the candidates as possible.

Always be on the lookout

In Chapter 6 I discussed that reality of candidates cheating on technical skills assessments, but that is not the only time you may come across "cheating". Some candidates will offer bold-faced untruths about their experience or even in rare cases about things like where they received their education or previous work experience.

One example, heard through the grapevine, is of a candidate who applied for a vice president level role at a major internet company. When asked what they had been doing in the time since they left their previous role, they replied that they had been traveling the world and when they needed some money, they would enter ML completions on Kaggle. Anyone who has competed on Kaggle would immediately know that that is a very poor strategy for dependable income. This person was not hired, as the experienced ML people on the hiring team knew to raise a red flag.

Your hiring team needs to be on the lookout for people who are exaggerating or straight up lying. If your organization does not have the in-house knowledge to vet candidates, you should bring in a third party that can help you.

When to do which interviews

Typically interviews either function as a part of sequence, where the candidate is assessed after each interview stage and a decision is made about advancing the candidate, or interviews are part of a stage in the sequence, in which the candidate will do several interviews before being assessed for moving to the next stage. It's probably most common for the onsite / final round to involve multiple interviews.

How you structure your interviews and where you place which interviews should be based on the funnel you expect to have, which is ultimately based on your resources and constraints, and the market. Additionally, you may want to put some interviews or interview topics very early in the sequence if the information is critical (e.g. the candidate being able to travel X% of the time may be crucial and should probably be learned at the application stage). As covered in Chapter 4, you typically want to spend an inverse amount of time per candidate relative to the stage they're in, i.e. you want to spend little time on fresh applicants and a lot of time on late stage candidates. This of course also comes down to your capacity relative to the supply of candidates. For high supply scenarios, such as junior roles, you are likely to have a larger supply than your capacity to do live interviews. For a lower supply role, e.g. a senior role or something highly specialized, you may be able to conduct live interviews for most if not all candidates. Refer back to Chapter 4 for more information.

The typical sequence is have a handful of screening interviews, before a more comprehensive final stage, consisting of multiple interviews covering several areas. The early stages allow you to gather more basic information, gauging whether the candidate meets basic criteria and allowing you to decide whether to advance them without your team or the candidate having to invest much time. The comprehensive stages allow you to reinforce earlier information and gain a more complete picture of the candidate's potential fit for the role, as well as giving the candidate a better understanding of the role.

This sequence works well for most situations, but you may be faced with scenarios where another structure makes more sense, such as spreading out the final stage into a series of interviews, e.g. when coordinating your team is not possible.

The following are examples interview sequences aimed at different hiring scenarios:

A typical low-to-mid candidate volume sequence

1. Resume screen
2. Recruiter screen (call)
3. First tech screen (online/call)
4. Hiring manager screen (call)
5. Onsite (with second tech screen) (onsite or virtual)

A high volume optimized sequence

1. First tech screen (online)
2. Recruiter screen (call)
3. Hiring manager screen (call)
4. Onsite (with second tech screen) (onsite or virtual)

A low volume sequence

1. Resume screen
2. Hiring manager screen (call)
3. Onsite (onsite or virtual)

What should you be assessing during an interview?

In addition to the technical skills previously covered, data science and MLE roles require other sets of skills, including:

- Team work
- Communication with co-workers, stakeholders, and customers of widely varying backgrounds
- Project management
- Technical skills related to process, design, and systems
- Professionalism

Your overall interview process should touch on these and other relevant skills, weighted in a way that fits the needs of the role. A consulting data scientist will likely need to be more "business savvy" and possess stronger communication skills than one that spends all of their time doing R&D, for example.

Interviewing strategy

Compared to many other roles, for data science and MLE, we have the luxury of being able to base much of our assessment on more objective – though by no means perfect – measures. That said, we still want to assess skills that are more subjective in nature, such as communication skills.

There are two basic ways to approach assessing skills such as communication: a dedicated interview or integrated into other interviews. To structure the entire interview process, how you assess such skills is an important decision point. The decision on that structure depends primarily on the relative importance of certain skills for the role in question and the constraints placed on you by candidate volume and your interviewing resources (e.g. people and time). As with the technical skills assessments discussed in Chapter 6, you are also faced with the fundamental tradeoff of the amount of time you spend interviewing a candidate and how complete of a picture of their skills and potential you can get.

Fads and snake oil in interviewing

There are a lot of interviewing techniques and tools the become popular, often for reasons that are not necessarily linked to their effectiveness. I will be the first to say that evaluating the effectiveness of interviewing techniques is very difficult to do, but there are some things that you see that are simply best avoided.

An example of this is "behavioral interviewing", a technique that has been popular in the past few decades. Behavioral interviewing is based on the reasonable sounding hypothesis that past behavior is the best predictor of future behavior. The interviews consist of asking the candidate how they handled past work scenarios. "Tell me about a time when X happened." The primary issue with this type of interview is that it relies heavily on the interviewer's ability to distinguish between true and fabricated stories[a], as well as distinguishing between candidate nerves and a true inability to answer well (this does also apply to technical interviews, to be fair).

Although common, candidates will often see these techniques as a sign of laziness on the part of the hiring company or simply an "ejection seat" to allow the company to safely reject them for vague reasons rather than based on merit. As a rule of thumb, if the interviewing technique has a trademarked name, requires paid training, or feels like a gimmick, it is probably best to steer clear.

[a]As you might expect, you can also buy some AI lie detection snake oil if you really want.

For a typical DS or MLE role, I think that professionalism, communication, and team work can be assessed in parallel with other focused interviews. For example, it's common to have a DS candidate give a presentation on a project as part of the interview process. This is typically a presentation that is heavy on technical information, but is also a chance to understand how and how well the candidate communicates technical concepts, how they structured their project, designed their solution, and how they adapt to the audience at hand.

Whether you choose to conduct interviews specifically for these skills and experience or as part of a more holistic assessment will depend on your needs, resources, and constraints. As with all parts of the hiring process, you made need to modify your strategy to meet the changing hiring environment.

Interviewing logistics and decision making

Once you have decided what types of interviews you want to do and how you will sequence them, the next order of business is planning interview logistics and the candidate decision process.

Basic interviewing logistics

Many things go into actually setting up and executing interviews well. Some basic things to strive for include:

- Making it clear who the primary contact person is for the candidate.
- If possible using a scheduling service to allow the candidate and your team to find the best times for calls and other interactions, rather than a long chain of emails.

- Explaining the hiring process early on to set expectations for the candidate.
- Promptly responding to questions and providing follow-ups.
- Interviewers recusing themselves from interviewing people they know. You want to avoid biasing yourself for or against people and also avoid (even the appearance of) cronyism or nepotism.

It's not always easy to move quickly, as there are typically many people involved in scheduling and making decisions. A large number of candidates compounds this. If you are transparent with candidates about why delays are occurring, they are typically understanding, but expectation setting is crucial. Sometimes conflicting timelines are unavoidable and you will lose candidates despite your best efforts.

The (virtual) onsite interview

When a candidate comes to your office or starts a day of virtual interviews online, you want the candidate to come away from the experience with a positive impression of your company and ideally a stronger desire to join your team. Of course you are primarily interested in discovering if the candidate is indeed qualified, will excel in the role, and make the team stronger overall. That puts you in a bit of a bind. You need to grill them to get as much data as possible to make a well informed decision, but also want them to have a good experience interviewing. To achieve both of those potentially conflicting goals, you want to design your candidate's interview day with both goals in mind.

Things you want in your process:

- Clear expectations for the candidate, including a schedule with interviewer names, topics, and specific expectations and preparation strategies, if applicable.

- Built-in breaks in the schedule.
- Water, snacks, and instructions on where the restrooms are for in-person interviews.
- A well prepared interviewing team.
- A clear point of contact for the candidate if they have questions or logistical / technical issues during the interview loop.
- Plenty of opportunity for the candidate to ask questions, meet people, and get a sense of the work environment.

Interview days, especially in-person ones, are long and tiring for candidates. Unless you are specifically trying to assess their endurance, you should try to make your interview day as short as possible. That said, you still want to give the candidate some amount of less structured time to interact with people and learn about your organization. A candidate lunch or dinner including people who are not part of the interviewer team is a common way to allow for a less structured flow of information. You should be explicit about times like lunch being more casual (for setting expectations of both the candidate and employees). Some candidates will ask a million questions and other may use that time to sit back and observe.

Dealing with mistakes you make

As with any human endeavor, you will inevitably make some mistakes during the hiring process, such as forgetting to schedule a call, sending a candidate the wrong email, or accidentally "ghosting" a candidate. What do you do in those scenarios?

The answer is: act professionally and do your best. Everyone makes mistakes. You should apologize and do your best to correct the error. Most candidates will understand.

Unfortunately, for many candidates their only interaction with an organization is through the hiring process and they may be quick to jump to conclusions based on single errors. You

> can't always prevent that, but you should still do your best to
> provide a good overall candidate experience.

On interview day, your team and the candidate will have potentially spent hours getting to know each other. At the end you need
to collect scores and feedback. This should be a structured process,
whether the feedback and scores are submitted via email, entered
into the ATS, or collected by the hiring manager. The sooner this is
done, the fresher the impression of the candidate in people's minds,
and hopefully the information will be of higher fidelity.

Decision making

Decision making in hiring is hard. Your goal should be to make it as
easy, fair, and unambiguous as possible. In Chapter 4, we discussed
several approaches and the various tradeoffs and pros and cons. The
most important thing is that you decide on a process, plan for that
process, and stick to it (up until you need to adjust it).

Should you give candidates feedback?

A question that comes up often related to hiring is how much
and what kind of feedback to offer candidates that you decline.
This is a tricky question for a number of reasons. In the US,
many companies are disinclined to give rejected candidates
feedback for fear that any information could be used in a
potential lawsuit, regardless of the merit. Hiring managers, on
the other hand, are often inclined to give people feedback.

The question then becomes: assuming you are allowed to give
feedback, what feedback should you provide? Sometimes candidates are rejected for purely logistical reasons (e.g. someone

else already accepted an offer). This is typically safe feedback to offer, but you still run the risk of angering a candidate that has put a lot of effort into their application and assessments. Other feedback is centered on the candidate's performance in the assessments and interviews. This can be useful for the candidate, but also can make them unhappy, as the inherent "noisy signal" nature of interviewing may make the candidate feel that they were treated unfairly.

Most candidates do not understand the realities of hiring from the employer side of things (e.g. the candidate may have done relatively well, but the pool of candidates is so large that they were not near the top). This makes it likely that many candidates will be unhappy with feedback, regardless of the accuracy and quality of the feedback.

Personally I tend to only give feedback when explicitly asked and try to give the candidate some context and expectations around what the feedback will be. All that said, I have been on the receiving end of useful feedback on occasion and found it very helpful. More often, I have received vague and useless feedback.

How do you know if your hiring process is succeeding?

The whole point of interviewing is to identify candidates that will perform well in the role and be a good fit overall. But how do you know if your process is succeeding?

As data scientists, our natural inclination to assess the performance of a process would be to identify a key performance metric, design a suitable experiment, collect data, and analyse the results. For most organizations this is not practical when it comes to hiring. The volume of hires is too low and the resources are simply not in place to do proper experimentation. Instead you are faced with more indirect measures and qualitative impressions, such as employee retention rates and performance scores, which give you a sense of how well the employee does, but not a strong sense of how changes in your process affect things.

That said, you can get a sense of the performance of your process by looking at those indicators. It is probably easier (and more painful) so see when your process is failing. Here are some of the things to look at when assessing your process:

- Are the promotion rates from one stage to the next in line with your plan?
- Do on-site interviewers complain about the quality of the candidates?
- How long does a typical candidate spends at each stage of the process?
- How much time is your team spending per candidate?
- How many candidates remove themselves from the process?
- How many offers are accepted?
- Explicit feedback from candidates[38].
- Feedback from your team about the parts of the process they're involved in.
- Retention rates, dismissal rates, and performance scores.

It's important to keep in mind that none of these are perfect indicators (e.g. a bad manager or environment can cause a good hire to leave quickly) and it's likely that you'll have no baselines to measure against.

---

[38]Understanding that candidates who are rejected are often inclined to offer less objective feedback on your process.

Summary

The goal of interviewing is for the team and the candidate to gain enough information to make well informed decisions. That is, of course, much more difficult in practice than in theory, but a strong process is possible.

The key takeaways from this chapter are:

- You need to have a strong understanding of your goals: which skills and experience you are looking for?
- How you design your process and sequence depends on your goals, resources, and constraints.
- Aim to spend a proportional amount of resources on a candidate relative to the stage / likelihood of making an offer.
- Train your team on how to interview and how to assess a candidate's performance in an interview.
- You want to design the process to be fair, welcoming, and as short as possible.
- Decide on a strategy for decision making, plan accordingly, and stick to the process.
- You will need to adapt your process as circumstances change.

Chapter 8: Setting up your team for success

The whole point of hiring a strong candidate is for them to help your team and the larger organization succeed. But hiring is only the first step in that process.

In this chapter, we will cover some of the topics that will help your new hires and the team to succeed in both the short and long terms.

Structuring your team

One key consideration when building a data science or machine learning team is deciding where the team should fit into the larger organization. While this is best decided at the genesis of the function itself, it's something that may need to be restructured as the internal demand for this function grows within the organization. A good time to revisit this is when you are deciding whether to grow the team.

The team within the larger organization

When a new field like data science comes into existence, there is naturally the problem of where to put that function within an organization. In the past decade a number of organizational models for data science and machine learning teams or individual contributors have emerged. I will not cover all of them, but a good, thorough overview can be found here[39], by Pardis Noorzad.

The placement and function of the DS or MLE team should be designed around the business goals of the larger organization and take into account the existing organizational structure.

Three common models for DS or MLE teams are the centralized model, the embedded model, and the hybrid model. Each has its pros and cons and works better for certain circumstances than others.

The centralized model

A centralized model (a.k.a. a center of excellence or consulting model) is a model where all of the data scientists and/or MLE's belong to a single, central team. They do their work as internal consultants to other teams in the organization, as external consultants working with customers, a centralized producer of insights, dashboards, and reports, or as a stand-alone R&D team (or perhaps a mix of those things). Depending on the overall function, they may fall under a different part of the larger organization, such as engineering, finance, product, etc.

This model has the benefit of all of the data scientists or MLE's being very well synced, while being able to provide some amount of DS and/or MLE capability to teams across the organization. This is also a good structure for organizations that need data science

---

[39]https://djpardis.medium.com/models-for-integrating-data-science-teams-within-organizations-7c5afa032ebd

related, long term R&D performed. A single manager can oversee this function relatively easily.

The drawbacks include the DS and MLE function being relatively isolated from the other functions and goals, difficulty moving successful R&D projects to production, and the other teams not having the chance to have their own core data science or machine learning capability. This model can often results in a series of proof-of-concept products, rather than first-class, data-powered products.

The embedded model

In the embedded model, the individual data scientists and MLE's are permanent members of other teams, such as engineering, product, or finance teams. They do not necessarily have a common manager and may not have a uniform hiring process across departments.

The key advantage of the embedded model is that teams in different parts of the organization can have their own long-term, core DS and/or MLE capability. This means that they do not need to coordinate or negotiate resources from someone else.

The disadvantages of this model include potential siloing of DS/MLE knowledge, potentially independent and inconsistent hiring processes, and added people management complexity for the manager, who has an additional specialized technical role under their umbrella.

The hybrid model

In the hybrid model data scientists and MLE's primarily work embedded on other teams, but still report to the manager of the organization-wide DS/ML team. Day-to-day work and project management falls to the managers of the teams the data scientists and MLE's are embedded in, whereas the DS/ML manager is responsible for hiring, professional growth, and people manager duties of those team members.

The advantages of this model is that function and product-based teams can have long-term, core DS/MLE capability, while knowledge is not siloed, hiring and professional advancement are standardized across teams, and there is a clear path for team members to move to other teams or projects.

Disadvantages include the added complexity of matrix style reporting and confusion about which manager is responsible for what.

What's best for your organization will depend on your specific goals and existing organizational structure. Of the three categories mentioned above, anecdotally some form of hybrid model seems to be the one where most teams end up.

Onboarding new hires

You want your new hires to succeed and make your team stronger. Onboarding is where that starts. Your newly hired data scientist is faced with the typical onboarding related to setting up all of their accounts, setting up their computing equipment, various HR-related tasks, and getting to know their new teammates. On top of that they need to get familiar with all of the various aspects specific to their roles: key initiatives, key metrics, data sources, deployment and monitoring systems, etc.

As with other technical roles, your new hire is likely to want to make real contributions as quickly as possible - hitting the ground running. Depending on the complexity of your infrastructure and other constraints, this may not be possible. Instead you need to focus on getting them up-to-speed as quickly as you can. To support this, you and your team should put effort into documenting your systems, including "getting started" or "golden path" material, designating people to help provide and maintain tutorials on your tools, systems, and techniques, and providing the new hire with ample time to explore and familiarize themselves with the environment and tools. Just as important, is making sure they know who to ask about what. One way to facilitate this is with an onboarding "buddy", who they are encouraged to ask any and all questions to. The scope of these supports will vary with team size, new hire volume, and complexity / novelty of your systems, tools, and techniques.

The process to set up basic "infrastructure" for your new hire, such as computer equipment and accounts, should start before their start date, such that they can get started as soon as possible.

A good practice to have in place is a short and midterm work plan for your new hire. A common form of this is the 30/60/90 day plan. For each time horizon, your new hire should have a concrete set of goals. Some example goals are:

- 30 day goals:
  - All equipment and accounts set up.
  - Meetings held with all key people the new hire needs to know.
  - Complete introduction "courses" for all key functions of the company (e.g. HR, product, engineering, data)
- 60 day goals:
  - "Hello world" usage of all relevant systems successfully completed.
  - First bugs / issues filed.
  - First small contributions, such as bug fixes or updates made.
- 90 day goals:
  - First non-trivial production contribution made.

In addition to all of the technical knowledge accumulation and work goals, you should also give your new hire the chance to simply get to know their new teammates and others within the org. In an in-person situation, this may start with something like a team lunch for the new hire. For remote work environments, this takes more intentional effort, such as setting up individual calls with team members or a virtual lunch, which is more awkward, but can have the more informal feel that helps facilitate people getting to know each more as people than just entries in their work calender.

Care and feeding of data scientists and MLE's

Experienced data scientists and machine learning engineers are in high demand right now[40]. With each month your new hire works for you, their market value increases. This means that you need to do your best to make staying in your organization an "easy decision" for your team members. You don't want to lose good people or incur the cost of re-hiring, if possible. In this section I'll cover some of the things that data scientists and MLE's are often looking for, or even expecting, in the work place.

Equipment and infrastructure

Data scientists and MLE's spend nearly their entire work day on their computers. Giving your team members a choice of equipment (e.g. a Linux, Mac, or Windows laptop, keyboard, mouse, monitors, desk, chair, etc) or even a budget to use as they see fit can help them be as comfortable and productive as possible.

Data science and ML typically require a broad range of software and infrastructure to do effectively. For both the effectiveness of your projects and the happiness of your team, you should strive to make access to tools and infrastructure as easy as possible. Having

---

[40]2021

to jump through lots of IT hoops to install software, access data, or deploy solutions is a sure way to slow down or kill projects and make data scientists and MLE's wonder if the grass is greener at the company that some persistent recruiter is trying to lure them to.

"Welcome aboard! No, we don't have any data..."

One of the classic mistakes when hiring data scientists or machine learning people is for the organization to either not have any data or to have data that is not accessible to the new data science team. What you typically see is a DS or MLE type person then spending months or longer working on data collection and/or data infrastructure implementation, rather than the work they are trained for and were hired to do. This is usually a recipe for failure, are the DS or MLE becomes frustrated and is easily lured elsewhere.

As discussed in Chapter 3, you should have some level of infrastructure in place before going down the route of hiring data science and machine learning people. In the extreme scenario, you should be informing your potential hire of the situation and your plan to get useful data flowing. This plan may involve a large effort from the new hire, but it should not be a surprise to them in any way.

Mission support

Data scientists are often portrayed as miracle workers, taking raw data and extracting business saving insights. This is, of course, a somewhat exaggerated version of the truth[41]. Your DS or MLE team needs to have the right support in place for accessing data

---

[41]OK, maybe this is in the category of hyperbole.

and deploying and maintaining models and other deliverables. This means that organizational buy-in and support needs to be in place, including specific support for servers, pipelines, etc. This may be in the form of specific team members (e.g. data engineers, web developers, devops, etc) or tools and platforms that are maintained by other teams specifically to enable and support the work done by data science and ML teams.

Skills and career development

Data science and machine learning are both vast, dynamic fields. State of the art, best practices, and tools are constantly changing. What this means is the data scientists and MLE's need to be constantly learning in order to keep up. Giving your team members the support they need to learn new technologies and techniques is not only good for their work, but also helps to keep them happy in their roles. Examples of support for skills development are:

- An education budget for purchasing books, online courses, and conference attendance.
- Internal lecture series.
- Internal journal clubs.
- Protected time for learning
- Hackathons (during work hours)

Related to supporting skills development is career development. Employees want to know what progress looks like and how they are doing. It's important to make the path for career advancement as clear as possible and to layout the criteria that employees need to fulfil to advance. While some data scientists and MLE's will be interested in moving into management[42], most will not. To support this, offering a technical individual contributor career

---

[42]If you do have someone who wants to move into management, I assume one of your first to do items will be purchasing a copy of this book for them.

path in parallel to the management path is important, as it allows individual contributors to continue to advance. These roles often carry titles such as "staff", "principal", and sometimes "fellow".

Autonomy, purpose, and trust

Data scientists and MLE's are highly skilled professionals. They want to feel valued and trusted at work. Nothing is worse than having your team put in a large amount of effort to build something and then have it ignored or discarded. Giving your team members the ability to be autonomous, while also giving them the support they need to carry out their work is key. Additionally, they must have a clear sense of why they are being tasked with what they are doing and how it fits into the big picture of what the organization is trying to accomplish.

Another aspect of team "health" is psychological safety. This means creating an environment in which your team members feel safe to take risks without the fear of being shamed for failure or of being embarrassed. This is very important in innovative and creative work, as ideas with uncertain outcomes must often be perused. As a manager, you need to model this behavior for your team and call out instances of psychological safety being violated. All of the goals in this section must be built on a foundation of mutual trust between the team members and managers.

Compensation and benefits

In a competitive market compensation is king, or at least pretty close. For experienced people, compensation is currently high and rising. To prevent your team members from being poached, you need to make sure that you are keeping up with the market. That often means making compensation adjustments that are not tied directly to performance, but rather to the larger trends in compensation. This goes for benefits as well. It's important to keep an eye on what your competitors are offering, as this is what they will use to try to woo your team members.

Summary

The goal of this book is to help you and your organization efficiently and effectively hire data scientists and machine learning engineers. But that is really just the start to having a successful data science effort. It's important to put your team in the best place in the larger organization to cultivate success. Additionally, you want to get your new hires up and running as quickly as possible and then support them in a way that allows them to do good work and feel valued.

Appendices

Appendix I: Task and skills breakdowns, with associated roles

This appendix breaks down common high-level tasks into skills. There is often a blurry line between the requisite skills and component sub-tasks, so some sub-tasks are listed here as well, or will be identical.

Task: Cleaning data

String manipulation	Collating or exploding documents	Data reconciliation
Expunging duplicates	Anomaly detection	Scripting data cleaning
Using cloud-based storage	Using cloud-based workers	Format conversion

Associated roles: data scientist, data analyst, MLE, data engineer, ML modeler, etc.

Task: Exploring data

Selecting subsets of data	Joining data by different criteria	Characterizing data distributions and correlations

Task: Exploring data

Visualizing distributions and correlations	Grouping and slicing data and displaying data by facets

Associated roles: data scientist, data analyst, MLE, ML modeler.

Task: Building data transformation pipelines

ETL	Scheduling processes
Deploying to the cloud	Monitoring pipelines

Associated roles: data engineer, data scientist, MLE.

Task: Formulating metrics

Working with stakeholders to identify the most important goals and considerations for measuring performance	Weighing the tradeoffs of candidate metrics
Determining the best way to present the metrics	Scripting the calculation of metrics

Associated roles: data analyst, data scientist, MLE, ML modeler, product analyst, product data scientist.

Task: Creating reports

Writing up results	Creating relevant visualizations
Scripting report generation	Presenting the results to relevant stakeholders

Associated roles: data analyst, data scientist, product analyst.

Task: Creating dashboards

Creating relevant visualizations	Scripting KPI calculations	Scheduling KPI calculations
Designing the dashboard for easy digestion by users	Deploying the dashboard and requisite data pipelines or jobs	

Associated roles: data analyst, dashboard specialist, analytics engineer, data scientist, product analyst, product data scientist.

Task: Designing and interpreting experiments

Determining the objective of the experiment in conjunction with stakeholders	Determining the best experimental design and statistical tests	Data collection
Data analysis and testing	Visualizing and reporting on results	Scripting the collection, analysis, and reporting

Task: Designing and interpreting experiments

Presenting results to stakeholders

Associated roles: Statistician, product data scientist, data scientist, MLE.

Task: Developing predictive models

Determining the objective of the model in conjunction with stakeholders	Performance metric determination	Data collection and cleaning
Feature engineering	Model development, training, and selection	Reporting results
Scripting the data collection, featurization, training, and reporting		

Associated roles: Data scientist, ML modeler, MLE, statistician, ML researcher.

Task: Maintaining predictive models

Designing performance and data quality measures	Creating and deploying monitoring dashboards/reports/APIs	Integrating notifications
Error investigation and bug fixing for the models and systems	Ongoing model development	

Associated roles: Data scientist, MLE, ML modeler.

Task: Communicating with stakeholders (internal or external)

Organizing and leading meetings	Presenting to technical and non-technical audiences
Slide and document creation	

Associated roles: Data scientist, data analyst, product analyst, product data scientist, ML modeler, DS manager, MLE.

Task: Creating and deploying ML infrastructure

Working with stakeholders to understand requirements	Systems design for scale	Integrating cloud-based components

Task: Creating and deploying ML infrastructure

Deployment into the cloud	Creating dashboards	Deploying and automating data pipelines
Unix commandline	Transforming data	Building, deploying, and orchestrating containers

Associated roles: MLOps engineer, MLE, data scientist, DevOps engineer, data engineer

Appendix II: Skills of different roles

This appendix lists typical skills used by some of the common roles in the data science and machine learning field. While not exhaustive, these give a sense of the skill sets and overlap between roles / titles.

Generalist data scientist: This is the broadest role and may be responsible for everything from business intelligence to building, deploying, and maintaining machine learning solutions, depending on the needs of the organization. Because of this, the generalist data scientist needs to have a very broad range of skills. Typically they are stronger in some areas than others, as the breadth of skills is simply so large.

Role: Generalist Data Scientist

Using cloud-based workers	Scripting tasks	Unix command line skills
Scheduling processes	Automating data collection	Scripting the calculation of metrics
Scripting report generation	Determining the objective of a model in conjunction with stakeholders	Working with stakeholders on measuring performance
Slide and document creation	Organizing and leading meetings	Determining the objective of an experiment in conjunction with stakeholders
Presenting to technical and non-technical audience	Distributed data processing	Data collection
Designing and running A/B tests	Visualizing distributions and correlations	Weighing the tradeoffs of candidate metrics
Characterizing data distributions and correlations	Determining the best way to present metrics	Creating relevant visualizations
Determining the best experimental design and statistical tests	Spreadsheets	Using dashboard platforms
Selecting subsets of data	Joining data by different criteria	Grouping and slicing data and displaying data by facets
Collating or exploding documents	String manipulation	Format conversion

Role: Generalist Data Scientist

Expunging duplicates	Data imputation	Data reconciliation
ETL	Feature engineering	Model development, training, and selection
Building and deploying data pipelines	Instrumenting systems	Deploying dashboards and requisite data pipelines or jobs
Error investigation and bug fixing for models and systems	Deploying to the cloud	Containerizing projects for deployment
Monitoring pipelines	Creating integration tests	Designing dashboards
Studying academic literature	Creating academic material for conferences and publications	Converting prototypes into production ready code
Creating code tests	Creating and following code style guides	Performing code reviews
Designing and implementing API's	General computer programming	Managing software dependencies
Project planning	Using API's	Anomaly detection
Using cloud-based storage		

Data analyst: The data analyst is the more traditional role related to extracting value from data in most organizations. Their focus tends to be on exploring data, attempting to explain past events, quantitatively summarize the current state of affairs, and possibly forecast future events. More often than not, they are largely focused on using tools, such as spreadsheets and dashboard platforms. While they may not use general programming languages, they often have a good grasp of query languages, such as SQL. In some organizations, they may be referred to as "data scientists", although their role may be much narrower than that of the generalist data scientist described above.

Role: Data Analyst

Scripting the calculation of metrics	Scripting report generation	Working with stakeholders on measuring performance
Slide and document creation	Organizing and leading meetings	Determining the objective of an experiment in conjunction with stakeholders
Presenting to technical and non-technical audience	Visualizing distributions and correlations	Weighing the tradeoffs of candidate metrics
Characterizing data distributions and correlations	Determining the best way to present metrics	Creating relevant visualizations
Determining the best experimental design and statistical tests	Spreadsheets	Using dashboard platforms
Selecting subsets of data	Joining data by different criteria	Grouping and slicing data and displaying data by facets

Role: Data Analyst

Expunging duplicates	Data imputation	Data reconciliation
ETL	Designing dashboards	Anomaly detection

Product analyst / product data scientist: This role is focused specifically on the development and status of products. Depending on the need, the skills may be more aligned with the traditional data analyst or they may be using more "advanced" methods associated with data scientists or statisticians. Common tasks include formulating and monitoring product KPI's[43] and designing and running A/B tests on features or designs to see how they affect the product.

Role: Product Analyst / Product Data Scientist

Scheduling processes	Automating data collection	Data collection
Designing and running A/B tests	String manipulation	Format conversion
Deploying dashboards and requisite data pipelines or jobs	Error investigation and bug fixing for models and systems	Deploying to the cloud
Containerizing projects for deployment	Monitoring pipelines	Creating integration tests

---

[43]Key performance indicator

Role: Product Analyst / Product Data Scientist

Studying academic literature	Creating academic material for conferences and publications	General computer programming
Managing software dependencies	Project planning	Using API's
Using cloud-based storage	Scripting the calculation of metrics	Scripting report generation
Working with stakeholders on measuring performance	Slide and document creation	Organizing and leading meetings
Determining the objective of an experiment in conjunction with stakeholders	Presenting to technical and non-technical audience	Visualizing distributions and correlations
Weighing the tradeoffs of candidate metrics	Characterizing data distributions and correlations	Determining the best way to present metrics
Creating relevant visualizations	Determining the best experimental design and statistical tests	Spreadsheets
Using dashboard platforms	Selecting subsets of data	Joining data by different criteria
Grouping and slicing data and displaying data by facets	Expunging duplicates	Data imputation
Data reconciliation	ETL	Designing dashboards

Role: Product Analyst / Product Data Scientist

Anomaly detection

Analytics engineer: This is a newer role that has a large overlap with data engineering. The role is geared towards specifically supporting analysts' activities, such as providing data pipelines or deploying dashboards. This role is often filled by a former analyst, rather than an engineer with a software engineering or traditional data infrastructure background, as is often the case with data engineers.

Role: Analytics Engineer

Designing databases and data schema	Using cloud-based workers	Scheduling processes
Scripting the calculation of metrics	Scripting report generation	Working with stakeholders on measuring performance
Visualizing distributions and correlations	Determining the best way to present metrics	Creating relevant visualizations
Using dashboard platforms	Selecting subsets of data	Joining data by different criteria
Grouping and slicing data and displaying data by facets	Format conversion	Expunging duplicates
Data imputation	Data reconciliation	ETL

Role: Analytics Engineer

Building and deploying data pipelines	Deploying dashboards and requisite data pipelines or jobs	Error investigation and bug fixing for models and systems
Deploying to the cloud	Containerizing projects for deployment	Monitoring pipelines
Creating integration tests	Designing dashboards	Converting prototypes into production ready code
General computer programming	Managing software dependencies	Using API's
Using cloud-based storage		

Data engineer: This role supports the data and infrastructure for data related tasks, such as databases, distributed processing systems, and data pipelines. This is typically a more engineering focused role, but requires a strong understanding of the data and typical issues around data and the uses thereof.

Role: Data Engineer

Systems design	Orchestrating system components	Load testing
Determining service level agreements with stakeholders	Scripting tasks	Unix command line skills

Role: Data Engineer

Automating data collection	Distributed data processing	Data collection
Collating or exploding documents	String manipulation	Instrumenting systems
Creating code tests	Creating and following code style guides	Performing code reviews
Designing and implementing API's	Project planning	Designing databases and data schema
Using cloud-based workers	Scheduling processes	Selecting subsets of data
Joining data by different criteria	Format conversion	Expunging duplicates
ETL	Building and deploying data pipelines	Deploying dashboards and requisite data pipelines or jobs
Error investigation and bug fixing for models and systems	Deploying to the cloud	Containerizing projects for deployment
Monitoring pipelines	Creating integration tests	Converting prototypes into production ready code
General computer programming	Managing software dependencies	Using API's
Using cloud-based storage		

Machine learning engineer: A machine learning engineer is (currently) a broad role centered on creating production machine learning. In some organizations that can be focused exclusively on developing models and others it can be solely focused on deploying and supporting models in production. Most MLE's do a combination of model development, deployment, and infrastructure support.

Role: Machine Learning Engineer

Designing and running A/B tests	Determining the best experimental design and statistical tests	Designing dashboards
Determining the objective of a model in conjunction with stakeholders	Slide and document creation	Organizing and leading meetings
Presenting to technical and non-technical audience	Weighing the tradeoffs of candidate metrics	Characterizing data distributions and correlations
Feature engineering	Model development, training, and selection	Studying academic literature
Creating academic material for conferences and publications	Anomaly detection	Scripting the calculation of metrics
Working with stakeholders on measuring performance	Visualizing distributions and correlations	Creating relevant visualizations

Role: Machine Learning Engineer

Grouping and slicing data and displaying data by facets	Data imputation	Data reconciliation
Systems design	Orchestrating system components	Load testing
Determining service level agreements with stakeholders	Instrumenting systems	Creating code tests
Creating and following code style guides	Performing code reviews	Designing and implementing API's
Project planning	Designing databases and data schema	Using cloud-based workers
Scheduling processes	Building and deploying data pipelines	Deploying dashboards and requisite data pipelines or jobs
Deploying to the cloud	Containerizing projects for deployment	Monitoring pipelines
Creating integration tests	Converting prototypes into production ready code	Managing software dependencies
Scripting tasks	Unix command line skills	Automating data collection
Distributed data processing	Data collection	Collating or exploding documents
String manipulation	Selecting subsets of data	Joining data by different criteria

Role: Machine Learning Engineer

Format conversion	Expunging duplicates	ETL
Error investigation and bug fixing for models and systems	General computer programming	Using API's
Using cloud-based storage		

Machine learning modeler. This is a narrow machine learning role focused on developing models for use in production. Typically the deployment is supported by other team members, such as MLE's.

Role: Machine Learning Modeler

Determining the objective of a model in conjunction with stakeholders	Slide and document creation	Organizing and leading meetings
Presenting to technical and non-technical audience	Weighing the tradeoffs of candidate metrics	Characterizing data distributions and correlations
Feature engineering	Model development, training, and selection	Studying academic literature
Creating academic material for conferences and publications	Anomaly detection	Scripting the calculation of metrics

Role: Machine Learning Modeler

Working with stakeholders on measuring performance	Visualizing distributions and correlations	Creating relevant visualizations
Grouping and slicing data and displaying data by facets	Data imputation	Data reconciliation
Scripting tasks	Unix command line skills	Automating data collection
Distributed data processing	Data collection	Collating or exploding documents
String manipulation	Selecting subsets of data	Joining data by different criteria
Format conversion	Expunging duplicates	ETL
Error investigation and bug fixing for models and systems	General computer programming Using API's	
Using cloud-based storage		

Machine learning researcher: This is typically an R&D centric role, with an emphasis on developing cutting edge technologies, that may or may not be intended for production use. This role is often similar to an academic role, in that creating materials for conferences and publications is a common focus.

Role: Machine Learning Researcher

Anomaly detection	Automating data collection	Characterizing data distributions and correlations
Collating or exploding documents	Creating academic material for conferences and publications	Creating relevant visualizations
Data collection	Data imputation	Data reconciliation
Deploying to the cloud	Determining the best experimental design and statistical tests	Determining the objective of a model in conjunction with stakeholders
Determining the objective of an experiment in conjunction with stakeholders	Distributed data processing	Error investigation and bug fixing for models and systems
ETL	Expunging duplicates	Feature engineering
Format conversion	General computer programming	Grouping and slicing data and displaying data by facets
Joining data by different criteria	Model development, training, and selection	Organizing and leading meetings
Presenting to technical and non-technical audience	Scripting tasks	Scripting the calculation of metrics

Role: Machine Learning Researcher

Selecting subsets of data	Slide and document creation	String manipulation
Studying academic literature	Unix command line skills	Using cloud-based storage
Visualizing distributions and correlations	Weighing the tradeoffs of candidate metrics	

MLOps engineer: The MLOps engineer is charged with supporting the deployment, monitoring, and maintenance of production machine learning, along with the needed infrastructure. This is a specialized MLE role, though it's often filled by people coming from a more general DevOps background.

Role: MLOps Engineer

Building and deploying data pipelines	Containerizing projects for deployment	Converting prototypes into production ready code
Creating and following code style guides	Creating code tests	Creating integration tests
Deploying dashboards and requisite data pipelines or jobs	Designing and implementing API's	Designing databases and data schema
Determining service level agreements with stakeholders	Instrumenting systems	Load testing

Role: MLOps Engineer

Managing software dependencies	Monitoring pipelines	Orchestrating system components
Performing code reviews	Project planning	Scheduling processes
Systems design	Using API's	Using cloud-based workers
Working with stakeholders on measuring performance	Deploying to the cloud	Distributed data processing
Error investigation and bug fixing for models and systems	ETL	Expunging duplicates
Format conversion	General computer programming	Scripting tasks
String manipulation	Unix command line skills	Using cloud-based storage

Summary and Cheat Sheet

Managers hiring data scientists and machine learning engineers face a number of challenges:

- A specific, but often broad set of skills needed for these roles.
- Candidates have highly diverse educational and work backgrounds, making qualifications hard to pin down.
- An often overwhelming number of applicants.

The following steps are designed to help you create an efficient and effective hiring process.

Steps to effective DS/MLE hiring

0. Understand what data science and machine learning is. (Chapter 2)

1. Understand your business needs. (Chapter 3)
2. Understand the which roles you need and which skills each role needs. (Chapter 3)
3. Map out your hiring goals, resources, and constraints. (Chapter 4)
   1. Understand your available resources, timeline, etc.
   2. Based on market knowledge estimate applicant pool size (both cold and warm candidates).
   3. Choose your tradeoffs based on how efficient your process needs to be.

4. Create specific and descriptive job ads and titles. (Chapters 3 and 5)
5. Create effective online and phone / in-person screening questions. (Chapters 6 and 7)
   1. Online test for cold applicants should screen for basic DS/MLE skills with enough gradient to set a passing threshold.
6. Design recruiting and screening process based on chosen tradeoffs. (Chapter 4)
7. Ensure your new hires are getting the resources and support they need. (Chapter 8)

An example screening process for a generalist data scientist

1. Filter cold applicants with online basic skills test.
   1. Optional for warm applicants without clear skills.
   2. Test covering basic data manipulation, analysis, programming, and ML skills.
2. HR phone screen warm applicants and cold applicants that passed the online screening.
   1. Drop candidates that cannot meet basic availability and communication criteria.
3. Hiring manager phone screen for candidates that have passed the HR screen and a resume review by hiring manager.
   1. ~8 minute company and role overview.
   2. ~8 minute background info from candidate.
   3. 10 minute basic technical screen question.
   4. 5 minute open questions and explanation of next steps.
4. On-site (or virtual) interview.
   1. 30 minute meeting with HR and hiring manager to go over interview process, role, and more company info
   2. 30 minute presentation by candidate on DS topic of their choosing, including Q&A by DS team.

3. 30 minutes for general DS technical questions by DS team and allow candidate to ask any questions to the team.

4. 60 minute coding session to verify candidate's programming skill level.

5. 30 minute meeting with business stakeholders to present a broader picture of the company to the candidate and gather feedback on communication skills (especially for roles that interface with many stakeholders).

6. Optional 5 - 15 minute meeting with high level executive to excite promising candidates.

7. 15 minute wrap up with HR and hiring manager to answer any questions and discuss next steps.

Made in the USA
Middletown, DE
16 October 2021